THE AMERICAN

ANTHONY BELCHER

The American

Copyright © 2021 by Anthony Belcher

Published by Waterton Publishing Company

Rainy Thursday Books

watertonpublishing.com

ISBN 978-1-7347632-4-9

All rights reserved. No part of this book may be reproduced, stored, or transmitted by any means whether auditory, graphic, mechanical, or electronic without written permission of the author, except in the case of brief excerpts used in critical articles and reviews. Unauthorized reproduction of any part of this work is illegal and is punishable by law.

Because of the dynamic nature of the Internet, any web addresses or links contained in this book may have changed since publication and may no longer be valid. The views expressed in this work are solely those of the author and do not necessarily reflect the views of the publisher, and the publisher hereby disclaims any responsibility for them.

Anthony Belcher

I was born on December 20th, 1956, at Ellsworth Air Force base, located in Rapid City South Dakota, not far from Mount Rushmore. I would, in later years use this fact as a way to counter white coworkers whenever the conversation turned to patriotism and Black Folks seeming lack of it. I would brag that I was born on an Air Force base under the steely gaze of presidents Washington, Lincoln, Jefferson, and Roosevelt, ending with who could possibly be more American than me? This kind of banter on my part earned me the reputation of being an "Arrogant Nigger". The word "Arrogant" replacing the word "Uppity" which White folk commonly used in the fifties and sixties, to describe black folks that they thought were smarter than them.

1956 was a good year. In the world of entertainment, Nat King Cole is the first African American to host his own TV show. Elvis Pressley earns his first hit on the Billboard charts. "The Ten Commandments" is released in theaters. "Marty", starring Earnest Borgnine wins the Academy Award for best picture. NBC debuts its iconic Peacock Logo. In the world of American politics, playwright, Arthur Miller appears before the House Un-American Activities Committee in Washington, D.C. Dwight Eisenhower is reelected for a second term as president, and on the day, I was born the federal ruling Browder v. Gayle takes effect, leading

The American

to the United States Supreme Court decision that declared the state laws of Alabama, and the laws of the city of Montgomery that segregated public buses were unconstitutional, effectively ending the Montgomery Bus Boycott, and legal segregation in the United States forever.

My earliest memories begin with a plane ride that began in NYC and ended in the United Kingdom. I have very sketchy and vague memories, as I was only around three years old at that time. I remember there being lots of lights as we left and lots of lights when we landed. Amos Jr, who was about one at the time got air sick on the way over. We landed and were transported to what I know now was temporary military housing in a trailer park. One of the trailer park residents had chickens. I remember this because I was scared to death of them. I would stand in the doorway trying to spy were they were hiding before going outside to play, only to have them ambush me once I was out in the middle of the yard and chase me back into the house. I was terrified and have no real use for live chickens to this day. The other incident that sticks in my mind from that time was the night someone came into our trailer and robbed us. My mom was a few trailers over from us playing cards with friends. I remember watching him as he came into our trailer, too afraid to make any

Anthony Belcher

sounds. I watched in silence as he went through the drawers and cabinets. I watched him take some things from the dresser and then watched him as he walked out. Once he left, I ran to the friend's trailer where my mom was playing cards and told her what happened. Years later Mom would mention that they later found out who he was and reported him to the authorities.

We would be stationed in England for almost three years. I would start the equivalent of kindergarten and attend school there for about a year. I had a best friend that lived next door to us, and there were two twin girls who lived on the same street as me that walked me to school and back. My sister Pam would be waiting for me when I got home, and we would spend the afternoons riding the cobblestone streets on the red scooters Dad had brought for us that summer. I remember Mom taking us to Rugby games, dog races, or to the nearby lake where we watched the rowboat races. I got a real kick out of the guy calling cadence from the back of the boat through a bull horn. There is a picture of Myself, Pam, and Amos, we were probably ages five, four and three at the time. I remember that we went to a professional photographer who had a studio in an upstairs flat. While we waited Amos Jr. got too close to an old metal radiator and burned his arm. In the picture you can see the crescent star

The American

shaped burn on his left forearm near his elbow.

Once we were finished with the photo shoot we left. We stood on the street waiting to cross to where we would catch the bus back home. For some reason I darted into the street just as a big red double decker bus was coming from the opposite direction. I made it across filled with glee at the excitement of dodging the bus. I thought it strange that I seemed to hear my mother screaming as I was crossing. I couldn't see her and the others because of the bus that had screeched to a stop, and I began to worry. The bus pulled away and I could see my mother standing on the other side of the street with her hands covering her mouth, and her eyes wide with panic. Then our eyes locked, and I watched as the joy and relief in her eyes turned to that look that all kids recognize from their mother that says you are in trouble. When they got to my side of the street I was hugged then slapped upside the head as she reminded me that I knew better than to run into the street.

The next big outing in England was our trip to the Zoo. We were fascinated by all of the animals we saw but seemed to be especially excited when we saw the giant turtles. My brother Amos, who was so fascinated by the reptile house that when we

Anthony Belcher

got ready to leave, we realized he wasn't with us and had to go and find him. When we found him, he was standing in front of a python caged seeming to be in total awe of the size of the snake. I remember the English people were nice and polite to us and we were commonly referred to as the Americans when we were out and about. When I started school, I was introduced to the class as the American. That was my identity. That's who we were.

One day Dad came home and said he had been given a new assignment. We were leaving England and headed to some place called Omaha Nebraska.

He slaps her. She responds "You Motha Fucka", then something crashes against the wall. I lay in my bed trembling. I can hear my younger sister Pam and brother Amos whimpering across the room. We all lay in our beds in terror. None of us speaking or acknowledging in any way what we were hearing. Pam, Amos, and I would all be adults before we would acknowledge to each other what we saw and heard throughout the years. Susan Summers would write about this phenomenon amongst siblings that grow up in Alcoholic homes not acknowledging the horror of it to each other in her book titled "Secrets" I hear the words from my father that signal that the fight is all but over. When I think

THE AMERICAN

back now, we never knew what they were fighting about. What we did know is that the fights came almost always after they had been drinking. As my siblings and I lay in the bed to afraid to even comfort each other, the signal that the fight was all but over came in these words from my father. "You had a baby on me. You need to tell that boy the truth".

These words though soothing because they signaled the end of their fight, also left me feeling shameful and guilty because I knew that I was the boy he was speaking of, and I was the reason for their fights. I would lay there in the dark looking over at my brother and sister, noticing that I was a shade darker than they and my hair was a little nappyier than theirs. With these thoughts swirling around in my mind, I would eventually find my way back to sleep. The next morning, we would all get up and act as if nothing had happened. I would catch them stealing glances at me and knew that they had gone to sleep with the same thought as me. What could I have possibly done to cause my father such anger? After all I was only seven years old.

My Dad's new base was Offit, which was home to the United States Strategic Air Command headquarters. I would find out later after my grandmother Belcher passed that Dad's job

Anthony Belcher

in the Air Force was a supervisor in the electronic department. During my own time in the service as a Pickup & Delivery driver, I regularly delivered sensitive electronic parts to the same departments that were located in hangers near the flight line.

There were numerous pictures of Dad having various ranks throughout his time in the service. Indicating that he was having trouble with Alcoholism throughout his twelve-year Air Force career. This is evidenced by the many pictures I found in my grandmother's bureau of him with different ranks. He would make Sgt., Staff Sgt, only to be busted back to Airman first or Airman second. I believe the last time they wanted to bust him down to Airman basic which would have drastically lowered his salary, which prompted him to decide to leave just seven years before being able to retire. He could've made the rank back. Looking back, I think it is reasonable to assume that Dad had reached that point in his addiction where the Air Force was getting in the way of his drinking. Just as I would some thirty or so years later when I decided that anything that got in the way of my smoking cocaine had to be removed from the equation.

My aunts and uncles all bragged about how dad was a high school valedictorian and tested as one of the smartest high

The American

school seniors in the state of Alabama the year he graduated. Many years later I would ask Dad why he never went to college. His two-word response was so coldly matter of fact that I felt a real sadness for him. His answer? "I couldn't".

Dad graduated high school in the nineteen forties. At the time black students who grew up in Alabama were not allowed to attend any of the state universities and colleges. If there were scholarships offered from the HBCU systems back then, they were few and far between. Seeing the nonchalant manner, and recognizing the underlying anger, in which he responded would later provide me with invaluable insight into this man I would so desperately need to understand.

Dad would take us to the base a couple of times a year during family day. Amos Jr., Pam, and I would stare wide eyed with wonder and awe as we got an up-close look at the Jet planes lined up on the landing field. I remember how elated we were when they allowed us to board a C-130 transport plane. There were many souvenirs to take home, my favorite being the full-size American Flag that we hung on our bedroom wall. We all took pride in being in the Air Force. Amos and I often talked back then as I am sure many brothers do, about one day following in Dad's

Anthony Belcher

footsteps. I remember the flight back to the states from England and landing in New York City, where my Uncle Gilbert picked us up and he and dad drove us to FT. Wayne, Indiana. After a short stay in Ft. Wayne, where we picked up my Aunt Alberta and my cousin Ronnie, we then made the drive to Omaha. I remember Mom and Aunt Berta constantly complaining to Dad about needing to stop, for food, bathroom breaks, etc., and his determination to do so as infrequently as possible. Through the years Mom and Aunt Berta painted dad as being selfish and more concerned with his timeline, than their comfort. I now believe that Dad having grown up in Alabama understood that in 1960/61 America, a black family on the road traveling through Iowa and Nebraska was not that much less risky than it would be driving through Mississippi. Fortunately for us we made the trip with no incidents.

    As it would turn out, the three years we lived in Omaha would be our only experience of living a traditional middle-class lifestyle as it was defined at that time. Dad got up every morning and went to work., (I would learn later that on most of these days he was still drunk or hung over.) Mom was a stay-at-home mom, who had a sandwich and juice waiting for me when I returned home from Lothrop Elementary school in the early afternoon. In my eyes, my house and life were not any different from the kids

The American

on my favorite TV show "Leave It to Beaver". I remember my mother walking me to the school to register for classes earlier that summer. However, when September came around and the first day of school, just like the kids on TV, I was ushered out the front door and directed to join the long line of kids walking past my house heading to school, eight to ten blocks straight up Pinkney St where we lived.

Kids of that day were allowed a lot more freedom and subsequent responsibility than kids today. As kids we enjoyed the freedom to roam the neighborhood parks, and lakes on our own, despite being no older than six and seven years old. We would spend our days at Kountze Park located a couple of blocks from the house on Pinkney playing on the swings, courts, and board games that were easy to check out from the little office. It would be there, while playing my first game of basketball that I first heard the phrase "I will menstruate your nose" when it was directed toward me by another kid about my age. This led to my first fist fight. While I do not remember who won the fight, I do remember that I dd not go home with a nosebleed. We spent a lot of days at Carter's Lake engaging in the great Tadpole hunt. For whatever the reasons my brother and sister and I were fascinated by Tadpoles. Specifically, that they turned into frogs. We would

Anthony Belcher

literally have four or five mayonnaise jars, all glass back then, no plastic, fill them with water and seaweed, then add two to three tadpoles to each jar. In the morning we would rush outside to check on their progress and see if they really turned to frogs only to find that most had died. Leaving us with about a dozen jars of dead Tadpoles and one angry mother who was screaming about the stink.

When I look back at the time, we spent in Omaha I realize that maybe they were the best years of my childhood, despite the almost weekly drunken fights and those infamous words of my father. Dad usually arrived home from work and sat in his armchair reading the newspaper and chewing on the collar of his shirt until dinner was ready most evenings during the week. Mom would make dinner and set the table, then call us kids in. We ate dinner together in the dining room. After dinner us kids would return to playing and mom would clean the kitchen. Later that evening we would watch the latest shows on TV, "The Big Valley" was a favorite in our household, until bedtime when we were all ushered upstairs. We went to church most Sundays. The church we attended was located just two houses down from us, and the pastor and his wife were regular visitors to our house. Our next-door neighbors, the Hortons, who were friends of my parents

THE AMERICAN

whom they had met while we were stationed in England. We were an average American family who like the American families that made up many of the hit TV shows of the time.

Mom was a stickler for getting her kids to bed early. We were in bed by eight pm sharp on most nights. Subsequently we were always the first kids up and outside in the morning. The running joke was that Cookies kids were sent to bed before dark and were up outside playing before dawn. Of course during the summer months, she relaxed, and we were allowed to stay up until we feel asleep. We had an old-fashioned two-story house with a big screened in front porch. During the middle of the summer when the heat got to be intolerable in the house, Mom would allow us to make pallets and camp out on the porch. The porch had a big stoop in front where we spent hours playing "Concentration" which was a word game taught to us by my older sister Sheila. It was in the house on Pinkney that while playing in the living room the Sunday after JFK was shot, I heard my mom scream "Oh my God, they shot that man", causing me to turn around just in time to see Lee Harvey Oswald rushed out of the police station into a waiting car.

Television would play a huge role in my developing mind.

Anthony Belcher

In 1964, TV had only been a staple in the home of most Americans for less than ten years. Mom often tried to explain to us kids how enjoyable it was to listen to tv shows on the radio. How great it was to use your imagination to see the action they were describing. My Uncle Bobby, also a big fan of the old Radio, could recite the entire promo for the Lone Ranger, and the Shadow, two of his favorite shows. I thought that having to imagine what the characters in the show were doing when you could simply watch what they were doing didn't make any sense. How could anyone enjoy a show they could not see. Besides radio was for listening to music in the red and white 57 Buick my dad drove.

As I grew up TV would become my major escape vehicle, and source of information. I have warm memories of the Friday nights watching "Burkes Law", with mom. "Merry Melodies", a cartoon show that came on every afternoon, followed by the "Mickey Mouse Club." Dad was a big Wrestling fan, and he would watch the matches every Wednesday night. I even remember the Midget wrestling matches which seemed to crack him up more than the other matches.

Along with the Kennedy assassination there are two other distinct incidents that are burned into my memory from that time.

THE AMERICAN

One such incident occurred as I ran through the living room and happen to hear from the TV a then really young Cassius Clay bragging to Archie Moore how he was gonna wup him so bad that after the fight he would make him kiss his feet. I thought that it is funny and stopped me in my tracks and stood there mesmerized in front of the old Philco. The other memory that sticks out is when Dan Rather aired his documentary on the nation of Islam introducing the world to Malcolm X. I am sure that part of the reason these two images mesmerized me was that seeing black people on tv was novel at best during those times. However, the sheer magnitude of these men's character was so powerful, I was frozen in my tracks by their image as if caught in a space age tractor beam and riveted in place. All of these shows and images would play important roles in the attitudes I would adopt as a man.

I know now, having wrestled with my own substance abuse and underlying issues, that the emotions Dad was dealing with had to be tough and ultimately affected his belief systems regarding right and wrong. Until this day neither he nor my mother has had a real conversation with me about how I came to be. What I do know from others is that he did not know she was pregnant when they married even though they married in October

Anthony Belcher

of 56, just two months before I was born. He was a young man in his mid-twenties. She was 19. He was her second marriage, and I her fourth child. He swore to the day that he died that mom was his first and only love. This is evidenced in the birthday cards he would send her every year, and anniversary cards he would send on their wedding anniversary until the day he died. By that time, they had been divorced and had led separate lives for over 40 years. He would sober up in the late 70s and remain sober until his passing in 2008.

Dad could never be described as a cuddly father figure by anyone's stretch of the imagination. He was a disciplinarian in general and came from a generation of men who believed that children should be seen and not heard. I was afraid of him and had been afraid of him for all of my short life. Yet, there were moments when he was a loving caring dad. There was the time he came home from work with a puppy for us kids. A little black and white puppy that we named "Toby Tyler" after a character in the latest Disney movie. I, being the oldest, taking care of Toby was my primary responsibility. Dad would also take us on fishing trips. There were grand cook outs in the summer with other families and their kids. My favorite times, by far were the family trips to the drive in. I remember getting a big kick out of

The American

Dad's comment about Sidney Poitier's movie "A Patch of Blue", looking more like A Patch of Black to him. After one day spent at the lake we got home and found Toby Tyler on the porch dead from a broken neck after being hit by a car. I cried so hard that my parents let me sit up front with them that night at the drive in where we saw Elvis in "Blue Hawaii"

Dad's specialty was Christmas. He would spend half the night laying out the perfect Christmas scene. I loved coming down the stairs to find the tree, all decked out with bulbs and blinking lights, casting dancing shadows throughout the house of the shiny new toys which were opened and displayed as if Santa had carefully set them down for us. There was always a half drank glass of milk and a partially eaten piece of cake added to complete the fantasy. To this day Christmas is my favorite time of the year. I believe Christmas was a special time for Dad as well. I don't remember he or mom doing much drinking during the Christmas holiday, and subsequently have no memories of them engaging in any drunken fights.

Dad loved my mother, and he loved his family, however, I can only imagine the deep conflicting emotions that consumed him when he looked at me. The feelings of love, betrayal, anger,

Anthony Belcher

and shame he must have felt when he looked at what for all practical purposes was his eldest son, had to be overwhelming. In my own recovery process, I would have to find a way to break the emotional shackles that had me convinced I was bad and unworthy because I wasn't my father's son.

I would learn from my 12 step experience the principle "That is better to understand than to be understood". It was and is through this principle that I have been able to break those shackles and move on from those feelings.

Back then, I was just a little boy who was sure that it was his fault that his daddy didn't love him. While I understand today that Dad was not a monster, but instead was dealing with his own conflagration of conflicting emotions. Dad was the kind of alcoholic who turned mean spirited and cruel when he was drunk. It would be during these periods that, he became the monster in my young life.

My feelings for dad during those times were painful and confusing. I hated him. I was afraid of him. At the same time, I wanted so badly to please him and be worthy of his love. I would get angry because I couldn't understand what I had did to him. Then I would immediately feel guilty for getting angry. Then I

THE AMERICAN

would get angry for feeling guilty. It was a terrible merry-go-round of emotions that I would have to make peace with as I grew into a man.

One summer evening Mom and I were up watching TV. Pam and Amos were upstairs asleep. I forget what movie we were watching. but remember the warm feeling of just hanging out with my mom. I relished having her all to myself. Suddenly there was a booming knock at the back door. Both Mom and I jumped from the couch and went to the big picture window that looked over our driveway and garage. There was no one there. Then there was knocking on the dining room windows. Then a knock at the front door. We stood their hugging each other. There was a noise coming from their bedroom which was off the living room next to the bathroom. Someone was in the house. I believe mom grabbed a knife and I hid behind her skirts peeking around her with wild eyes. Dad jumped out of bedroom and screamed Boo! We could tell he had been drinking and as unfunny as he was, we knew he hadn't crossed over to fighting mode, and went to bed.

There would be a fight a few nights later after they had had friends over to drink and play cards. Pinochle was the card

Anthony Belcher

game they played. They played cards and drank well into the night. After everyone left the fight began. This fight seemed to be more intense and lasted longer than what was normal. It was a dozy! Instead of cowering in our beds that night I lead Pam and Amos into the street and next door to wake up the neighbors. We were all crying and screaming.

Joyce Horton walked us back into the house. Dad exploded, maybe because of embarrassment of having Joyce being there, he began screaming at us to get back upstairs and go to bed. We stood at the top of the stairs crying, whimpering, and clutching each other. He threw a boot up at us screaming for us to shut up and go to bed. I remember looking at the boot totally amazed that it had landed standing upright and stood there in front of us swaying a little. We went to bed expecting to get up the following day to whatever mess they left. Half drank beers, half glasses full of liquor. Ashtrays full of cigarettes.

Only this morning was different. Dad was up already up and cleaning the house. Mom called us all into their bedroom where she told us to get some things together because we were going to Ft. Wayne to see Grandma. While we packed, Dad for some strange reason began setting up his barbeque pit. I remember

The American

complaining to Mom that I didn't want to go to Ft. Wayne. She said I had to. As we drove away in the big yellow taxi, I looked out the back window with tears running down my cheek at my dad standing all alone in the driveway.

We boarded the train to Ft. Wayne and after a few hours Pam, Amos and I were singing the popular songs of the day with three nuns. It could have been a scripted scene out of a movie. Three little black kids and three white nuns hamming it up for a train car full of people. This kind of thing wasn't uncommon for us when we were out in public, most likely due to the three of us still having some semblances of a British accent. Amos and Pam had developed most of their vocabulary while we were living in England and their accents were still pretty thick. Pam, who was and is very fair of skin had a natural blond streak in her hair. Even at this young age we felt different because of how we looked and spoke. Sometimes these encounters were pleasant as with the nuns, not so much when a year or so later after we had moved to Ft. Wayne, one of my teachers called me a liar when I wrote about the summer, I visited the London Zoo.

To the average White, and for that matter Black American, we were a curiosity act with our British accents, proper and

Anthony Belcher

manners. We stayed in Ft. Wayne for a couple of weeks, then William and Joyce Horton, our neighbors, came and picked us up and drove us back to Omaha. It was the summer of 1964, and as it turned out it would be our last in Omaha.

It was a memorable summer. Dad was assigned temporary duty in Viet Nam, my two older sisters Sheila and Cindy from my mom's first marriage came to visit that summer. Right before Dad left for Viet Nam, my Grandparents visited and brought Greg and Denise, Mom's younger brother and sister, who were our age. Greg nine months older than me and Denise four months younger to spend a couple of weeks with us. My brother William who had just been born in March the year before was a "walker" baby. As the summer began Mom had a total of eight children in the house all to herself. Sheila was the oldest at 13, with Cindy, a year behind her, Greg was 9, Denise and I 8. Followed by Pam who was 7, Amos Jr. 6, and baby William 1. Needless to say, she had her hands full.

Within the first couple of days they were there, Greg and I were playing with Mom's portable tape player and broke the switch. We were not trying to break it, but we knew as soon as we did, that Mom was going to beat our asses. She had made it clear

The American

to all of us that under no circumstances should any of us touch her tape player just a couple of days before. After we all get home later that day Mom discovered the broken tape player. Sheila and William had been with Mom, so they were in the clear. The girls, Cindy, Denise, and Pam had been off at the park that day and had no alibi. Greg and I, of course feigned complete innocence. We had no idea what had happened. Now in those days it wasn't uncommon for a parent to come to the conclusion that since we kids would lie for each other, that if no one stepped forward to claim responsibility, all would share in the punishment. She lined us all up in the dining room and began to ask us one by one what we did that day. During the interrogation, the girls admitted that they had come in and looked at the tape player but hadn't touched it. We all knew that they, admitting they looked but hadn't touched the tape player wasn't likely. Greg and I continued to deny any involvement with the tape player at all. Something about all five of us standing there looking and claiming innocence tickled Mom. This happened regularly with my mom and how she disciplined. It was a style of parenting that she learned from her mother and grandmother.

A few years later after we moved to Ft. Wayne Greg, and I were upstairs jumping on the beds. We were doing back flips,

Anthony Belcher

front flips and having ourselves a time. After having told us to stop a gazillion times my Granny came up the stairs, armed with the "Pancake Turner", as we called her spatula, and caught us in mid jump. She instructed us to pull our pants down and lay on the bed so that she could give us our whuppin. We looked at the floor. Then looked up at each other. Then we looked at her and with all the earnestness we could muster, shook our heads vigorously back and forth No! She was taken aback and said what? We again shook our heads No! She laughed her hardy laugh followed with an "I'll just be damned". Without warning she knocked us both over on the bed and whacked us two or three times each, across the butt with the pancake turner.

Mom, now looking at all of us, while trying to stifle a laugh, called us a bunch of liars, and sent us to bed. The next day Greg, Denise, I, Pam, and Amos, whom we called June bug all set out for Carter's Lake armed with a couple of mayonnaise jars each. We were going to catch some Tadpoles! We had a nice little spot under a big tree where we would scoop the tadpoles out and put them in our jars. Denise who was scooting her chair along the little wooden bridge nearby ending up in the lake. We all stood at the edge telling her that she had better get out of that water cause momma was going to get her. Denise was dog

The American

peddling to stay above water but wasn't moving forward. Then there was a big splash where one of the teenaged boys from the neighborhood dove in and pulled her out. She had fallen into a deep part of the lake and was possibly in danger of drowning. The big kid pulled her out, as we scolded her. She stood there soaking wet from head to toe, trying to hide her fear. For some reason this tickled us, and we all burst out laughing. We marched back home tadpole less and wondering how Mom was going to react to this bit of news. Greg and Denise would head back to Ft. Wayne after a couple of weeks, and Mom gave us the great news that Sheila and Cindy were going to live with us permanently.

Mom had been telling us stories about Shelia, Cindy, and Baby Dennis, as he was called, for as long as I can remember. They were my older siblings from her first marriage. Shelia and Cindy lived with their grandmother and grandfather in Beckley West Virginia. Dennis who would have been referred to in today's world as medically challenged, my mother told us in the language of the day was born retarded and lived in a home in Mansfield Ohio where my Great Grandparents lived. I didn't really understand what "Retarded" meant but it was always followed with, he, Dennis, who would've just turned three when I was born, taught me to talk. I figured in my young way of thinking that retarded, whatever

Anthony Belcher

it meant couldn't be that bad if he could teach somebody to talk. Throughout the years, Mom rarely talked about him. He wasn't a secret; he was more like an afterthought. We met Sheila and Cindy for the first time when we returned from England during our short stay in Ft. Wayne. I wouldn't meet Dennis until I was sixteen. While Sheila, Cindy, and all of us would become as close as any siblings that all grew up in the same house, Dennis would be absent from family get-togethers for a major part of his life.

Having two big sisters around was cool. Sheila who is five years older than I, was a great big sister, and at the time I thought the most beautiful girl in the world. The first day she arrived we told her about the older girl who made it her business to bully us whenever we were headed to the lake or the local convenience store. My big sister put an end to that nonsense the very next day when she asked us to show her the way to the store. Off we went, only she trailed a little way behind us. I don't remember the girls name, who was bullying us. Only that she was a few years older than me. Just like clockwork she popped out of her yard and started in on us. She was very surprised when Sheila, who was a few years older than her came up and informed her that continued harassment of her little brothers and sisters would not be a healthy endeavor for her moving forward. I don't know if

The American

it was Sheila's very pronounced West Virginia twang or the calm and even toned manner in which she promised this young lady that she would kick her ass. either way it worked. The girl got the message and never bothered us again.

I was the stereotypical pest of a little brother and made it my business to find new ways to irritate Sheila constantly. It was during laundry day one Saturday afternoon that I finally managed to hit the breaking point of her patience. Mom had the old-fashioned washing machine with the rolling pin type wringer and still hung clothes out to dry on the close line in the back yard. She also used a big mettle wash tub where I believe she soaked and rinsed certain items before putting them in the washer. Sheila was on tub duty that morning and I was up to my usual attempts to irritate her. I believe I was pulling her hair, poking her or both trying to get her goat. She kept telling me "Stop it Tony", in her soft West Virginia drawl. After the third or fourth time she told me to stop, I went to poke and ended up sitting in the rinse tub, with wet clothes thrown in my face. My Mom heard the commotion and came in from the kitchen and asked, "Sheila, what did you do to that boy", and she replied in such an innocent manner, "Nothing Momma" that for a minute I, wasn't sure how I got in the tub myself.

Anthony Belcher

My other sister Cindy became my buddy and protector. At that point in her life Cindy was still more flat chested little girl, than budding young woman that Sheila was. There was a boy of about my age who wanted to fight me. I didn't want to fight. My big sister Cindy wasn't having any of that and made sure that I did. When I lost the fight. She walked me home telling me it was okay. She told me that I was still a winner because I stood up for myself. Yep, having two big sisters in my life now was pretty cool.

I was sitting on the front porch enjoying the afternoon sunshine when I hear a disturbing noise. I look up and see one of the older boys barreling toward me on his Schwinn with my five-year-old brother Amos sitting between the handlebars. They skidded to a stop, and June jumped off yelling they are fighting the police at the park. The older guy sped away in the opposite direction of the park, and June ran into the house to tell Mom. About that time two guys in their late teens ran past me with four of Omaha's finest right on their tales. One of the officers threw his Billy club striking one of the teens square in the back. He buckled but did not fall and continued to run away.

Mom and the rest of the kids came running out of the house as two squad cars screeched to a stop right in front of the

The American

house. Mom started to usher kids onto the porch. A brick hits one of the police cars and knocks the cherry off the top. Another brick hits one of the cops smack in the face. There's a man in his mid to early twenties fighting desperately with two, then three cops until they finally get him to the ground and cuffed. Another brick is thrown hitting another officer then all hell breaks loose as one the officers let off his shotgun. Mom usher's all of the kids upstairs, where we line up and watch the action from bedroom windows.

Squad cars are pulling up from all directions with cops jumping out of them with guns drawn. The five or six guys that didn't get away are ushered into a Paddy wagon and driven away. The fighting doesn't stop there as we can hear sirens and gun shots from nearby blocks well into the night. As quickly as it started, it ended with all of the squad cars screeching away, sirens wailing in different directions. As the sound of the sirens faded away, we all filed back downstairs, through the dining room into the living room where we were all shocked to find baby William sitting in his walker spreading the remainder of his spaghetti dinner on his face. He had sat there eating throughout the whole ordeal.

I doubt if the incident in Omaha made the national news

Anthony Belcher

in that summer of 64. The riots in Harlem New York would get all of the attention that year setting off a decade of riots to follow in major cities across the country. Ironically enough, The Harlem situation would kick off just two weeks after President Johnson would sign into law the Civil Rights Act. America was starting to boil, and these incidents were only the beginning of a decade that would be later defined as the "Turbulent Sixties".

The remainder of our summer was filled with wonderful days of staying up late to watch old movies, one of our favorites being Huckleberry Finn. We really enjoyed it when the tattletale cousin finally gets slapped by Aunt Poly. One Saturday afternoon, I remember watching in wonder as Cindy and Sheila went absolutely nuts screaming and crying while watching "Little Anthony and The Imperials" on the "Mike Douglas Show". I remember sitting there and thinking how stupid girls were. The best times were when Sheila would take us all to the movies. We really went in for the new horror movies that had come out that summer. The Horror movies of the mid Sixties when compared to today's fair of guts and gore, not only look fake now, but they also appear really corny. However, at the time we loved them. Vincent Price in "House on Haunted Hill" was one in particular one of the scariest. I watched this movie a few months ago, and laughed hardily at

The American

the scene, that back then gave us all nightmares. The scene was where this dead person climbed from the pool of acid looking as frightening as the science class skeleton. He chases the men and women characters, who run away screaming until one of the women falls and the skeleton caught up with her. Looking back, I often wonder how we could be so scared by something that now looked so fake and non-scary. It remains that at that time ole Vincent and Christopher Lee as "Dracula" sufficiently scared the beejeebees out of us.

As the summer ended, Mom began the process of getting Sheila and Cindy registered for school. They would both attend Horace Mann Jr. High located across the park from Lothrop Elementary. We all looked forward to walking to school together and settled in for the coming year. About two weeks before school started, we got a surprise visit from Sheila and Cindy's grandmother and a couple of their uncles. They visited with mom for a short time before suggesting that they needed to go to the corner store to pick up some things. They also offered to buy ice cream for us kids. Amos and I were selected to ride along, and we got into the car with Sheila, Cindy, her grandmother, and two uncles. When we got to the store one of the men gave me some money and said for Amos and me, to go into the store and by the

Anthony Belcher

ice cream. When we came out of the store, they were gone.

I don't remember us being overly alarmed initially. It was more like we were confused. The store was the same one we walked to all the time, so we just headed home looking for their car on the way. When we got to the house and their car was not out front, I think that it was then that we both started to feel that maybe something wasn't quite right. We went into the house and told Mom what had happened. At first, she too looked confused, then her face began to change. Slowly she sat/slumped down into one of the dining room chairs shaking her head and said, "Oh My God, They Took My Kids". She began to cry. Then she got angry. Through her angry tears she looked at me and Amos and said, "How did ya'll let them take my kids" By then we were all crying. Later that night as I lay in bed waiting for sleep. I felt a great emptiness in the house. I was already missing my sisters and certain that the reason they were not there, was my fault.

It would be over forty years before I asked Sheila about that time. She told me that there was a custody hearing during which she had to face a judge and choose between living with her mother and her grandmother. Sheila chose to stay with her grandmother because she did not want to leave Cindy behind,

The American

who's custody the Judge had awarded to her grandparents due to her age. In looking back at this now I estimate that Sheila and Cindy had been with their grandmother since before I was born. It is very reasonable to expect that their grandmother felt like she was only getting her kids back from a mother who had once abandoned them. I also realize that Mom, in her anguish was not actually blaming her eight and six-year-old sons for what had happened. That said, both Amos and I carried the guilt of that day into our adult lives.

Ruth Ann, "Cookie" Luckie, was born on January 16th, 1937, and raised by her grandparents Mabel, and Otis Ross in Mansfield Ohio, a small town located in the north central part of the state for the first ten or so years of her life. Grandpa Otis who served during WWI would work until retirement at the city jail as a janitor, Grandma Mabel, I believe did some domestic work and was a stay-at-home mom. My mother's stories paint them as a normal American family of the time. They went to church on Sundays. They ate meals together and gathered around the radio in the evenings to listen to their favorite shows. Grandma Mabel was a leader in the church, and Grandpa Otis had a jug stashed in the basement that he would ease down the stairs to visit on most evenings. Mom was the only girl in the house and was raised

Anthony Belcher

with her brother Bobby, her Uncle Clarence, and her first Cousin Jerome, Whenever Mom spoke of these times, and she did so often, her face would light up with joy.

Mom was married and pregnant with my oldest sister Sheila by the time she was thirteen. Cindy and Dennis came in stairsteps over the next two years. This seemed to be a pattern for the women in mom's family as both her mother and grandmother were married in their early teens. The story is that Mom and Gene, my older sibling's father, went to West Virginia shortly after Dennis was born, to get on their feet. I am guessing that this would be the period when Dennis was diagnosed and sent off to Mansfield. The situation in West Virginia, along with their marriage ended up not working out. Gene went to California and mom moved back to Ft. Wayne to get on her feet, leaving the girls with their grandparents promising that she would return or send for them shortly. Shortly, turned into that fall day of my third-grade year. Mom never talked a lot about her time in West Virginia in any detail. Mom didn't talk to us much about her growing up at all after her time in Mansfield. In later years she would tell me that she and the girl's grandmother had made up over the incident in Omaha and all was forgotten and forgiven. Me? Well, it would take a little longer before I could get there.

The American

The days following are pretty vague in my memory now. Pam, June, and I started school, and had begun to fall back into our routine. Dad returned from Vietnam a few weeks later. He brought back gifts for all of us. Something for mom. A doll for Pam, and little boats for June and me. Only a month or so would pass before we learned that Dad was getting out of the Air Force, and we were moving to Ft. Wayne Indiana.

I didn't know it then, but Dad and Mom's marriage was coming to an end and would be practically over within a couple of years. Without the Air Force to hold him in check, he would sink further and further into full blown alcoholism. Eventually becoming a gutter drunk.

My Grandparents Thelma, "Top" and "Dennis" Morris lived in a huge house with four big bedrooms upstairs and a monstrous bathroom. The kitchen like the bathroom was humongous. The kitchen had two doors to the outside. The back door opened into the back yard directly behind the house. The side door looked out into that was bordered by the driveway. Form this door you could see straight down Cedar Street. In the summers the firefly's, (lightning bugs to us), would fill the yard with what appeared to be a thousand lights. It would be this door that Granny would

Anthony Belcher

call us from when the streetlights came on. Letting us know it was time to come into the house. In the basement was a furnace room and a coal bin. Greg and I were often called upon to go downstairs and throw a couple of shovels of coal in the furnace during the winter months. There was a big back yard with a cherry tree, and the family dog Pretty, a full bread collie guarded it all from her little house in the back. My grandfather worked for the railroad and ran numbers. Even though there were three adults and six kids in the house with my little Sister Tracey on the way. I don't remember the house feeling cramped, or crowded, as there seemed plenty of space to accommodate us all.

Granny was a character and the unchallenged matron of her household. Part "Big Momma" and part "Mae West" she would brag about the hole in her bedroom ceiling, as she showed us, "That's where I shot at your grandfather" with the same sweetness in her voice as she would when calling us to breakfast for some of those giant buttermilk pancakes, she made for us on Sunday mornings. She was a respected member in good standing at her church. She was also known for terrorizing an Electric company employee after he climbed the pole in front of the house and shut off our electricity. Watching her favorite show on TV when the electricity went off, she immediately ran into the kitchen and

The American

grabbed a meat cleaver then ran back through the house and out the front door.

There she stood at the base of the pole in her slip and bra, and meat cleaver in hand. With five kids clutching her slip, she promised the gentlemen in as colorful language as she could muster, (and boy, could she muster), that she would surely cut off some of his ASS when he came down from that pole. if he did not proceed to turn her power back on. She went on to chastise him for his unchristian ways and how unamerican it is that he would put a poor widow woman and her five kids in the dark over a few dollars for a bill that was only a few months behind. I imagine it was a good thing none of us kids new what a "Widow" was, or we might have spilled the beans that her husband was alive and well.

The poor man looking scared to death seemed to call someone on the phone and then sheepishly made his way down the pole and giving Granny a wide berth made it into his truck. Needless to say, our lights did not get cut off that day. Gramps went to work and did what he did every day coming home every night with bags of money. He would be the one we were sent to for Saturday matinee money where for fifty cents you could see two movies and get a bag of popcorn. We lived with them for a

Anthony Belcher

couple of years.

When we first moved to Ft. Wayne from Omaha, we lived in a house on Berry St. Mom worked at Wayne Candies which wasn't far from the house. Dad I believed worked at a small electric company. I remember there being a fight followed shortly with us moving to my grandparents. I believe this prompted Dad to try and get sober which he did for a short time. We visited him a couple of times in the little rooming house he lived in. I remember it being sort of strange because of his concentrated effort to be nice to us. His sobriety didn't last very long and shortly after my little sister Tracey was born; they would have the biggest scariest fight of all.

We were all across the street at the Robinson's house watching a movie. Dad knocked on the door and Mom went outside to the porch to talk to him. First the cussing came, followed by slaps and fist hitting flesh. Us kids immediately began crying and running across the street to my grandmother's house. The fight continued once inside Granny's with Dad chasing us all upstairs, then back downstairs. I came running down the stairs ahead of the others. Granny was laying on the couch and as I stood there not knowing where to go or where to hide, she pulled me onto the

THE AMERICAN

couch and hid me behind her. When dad came back asking where I was, she told him she didn't know. Someone had gone up to the numbers house and got Gramps and he came into the house about that time. They had a few words and then scuffled before Gramps picked dad up by his collar and back of his pants then threw him out of the house. Things quieted down for a minute, and dad apologized to Gramps. He then said he just wanted to talk to mom. She went out to talk to him carrying baby Tracy in her arms, none of us aware that he had a shotgun in the car. It wasn't long before the cussing and hitting began again and mom ran back into the house leaving the baby with dad. Dad screamed after her to come back or he would kill the baby. Realizing she didn't have the baby mom turned to go back outside to get her when we all heard the deafening sound of a shotgun blast.

For a moment everybody froze in silence. Mom began to cry hysterically. Gramps slowly opened the screen door and went outside. A moment later he returned with a scrawling but much alive Tracy. Someone had called the police and three to four officers arrived in a "Paddy Wagon" which was commonly used by police forces in those days. Dad did not try to resist the police, nor was he compliant. He was really drunk and in some sort of a daze. He had put the shotgun back in the car before the police arrived and sort of sat there on the bumper of his car looking at the ground as if he was not sure of what had just happened. When they tried to put the cuffs on him, I think he jerked away or made a sudden move. I am not sure if he did this on purpose or was too drunk to really understand their instructions. They reacted the way cops do and beat him up pretty bad right there in front of us. At that moment, watching them hit him with their billy clubs, I hated them much more than I hated him for what he had just done.

We would move shortly after that, to a two-bedroom apartment in a neighborhood known as Westfield due to it being located on the far west side of town. The apartment complex, known as the Village, was once used as military housing back in the forties when there was an Army base at Bare Field. These were the first "Housing Authority" units that were partially funded by the federal government and would be known today as low-income housing.

Many of the "Projects" located throughout small to midsized midwestern cities and towns turned old military housing into these low-income housing units, and when new housing was built, they were built in this style, as opposed to the high-rise

The American

buildings erected in the larger cities of the east, like New York, or big cities in the Midwest like Chicago. Our little apartment was located on Catalpa Street, the main drive that separated the two halves of the Village.

The apartments on the West side of Catalpa were occupied almost entirely by White families, and the East side of Catalpa occupied by Black families. Taylor street, the other main thoroughfare, along with a few other side streets, held houses that were mostly occupied by two parent Black families. Further to the west past Portage Jr. High school you would find your middle, upper middle, and rich white folk. On the east side of Catalpa and the north end of the apartments was the Kiwanis Branch Y.M.C.A. At the west end of Catalpa before getting onto highway 24 was Rock Hill Park.

Westfield was the type of neighborhood that was filled with kids. The Kiwanis Branch YMCA was the center of our activity where we would all learn arts and crafts as little kids and later would learn to play ball, go on summer trips to see the Cincinnati Reds, or Detroit Tigers play baseball. There would also be camping trips, and later, the Y would be where I would attend my first "Dance" which they hosted for teenagers. Because we were

Anthony Belcher

separated from the main body of black folk, who for the most part lived on the east side of town, we developed a special bond, and reputation so strong, that for many years after the projects were torn down, a group of families held annual Westfield reunions where many of the folks from the old days would show up.

I was ten when we moved to Westfield. On the surface I was a normal ten-year-old doing and thinking normal ten-year-old things. Underneath, on the inside I was a seething cauldron of anger, guilt, and shame. I had begun to search men's faces when we were out in the community at grocery stores and the like, wondering if maybe one was my father. I often daydreamed that maybe my father was a famous person, a pro athlete, or a famous musician. I had also begun to develop a serious resentment toward my brother Amos. He being named Amos, after Dad, when both of my father's brothers had named their oldest sons after them, had always bothered me. That Dad had given his second son his name instead of me, only served as a big red confirmation that I was a not my father's son.

Both Amos, and Pam and later William and Tracy were all of a lighter complexion than me. Their hair was straighter and in the black community not having these white people traits

The American

was considered ugly. Amos Jr was already proving to be a better athlete than me, and he got straight As in school, while I could only manage a few A's with the rest being B's and C's. In my perceptions, Amos Jr. got all of the shine even though I was the older brother. Worse than that was the concrete surety I felt that the reason he got the shine was because I was not worthy of any shine or special attention. I was bad. I was the reason my parents were getting divorced. I was the reason my daddy was a drunk. The shame I felt made me feel I had to be someone everyone liked, even though I felt that no one could really like or love me. Underneath this phony facade I presented to the world, I seethed with anger.

Shortly after we settled into our new apartment Mom lost her job, and we had to go on welfare. Having to use food stamps at the store was a total embarrassment for me, and I stated to avoid having to go. All of the furniture we had in Omaha was gone. The furniture we had now was propped up on "Commodity Cans", as they were called then. They were part of the overall welfare program. Before food stamps, food assistance was administered in the form of a truck that would come by on a regular basis with canned foods. Everything, meats and vegetables all came in big white cans, the contents of the cans was written in bold

Anthony Belcher

black font on the front of the can. The "Potted Pork" we would not eat, I think because there was a lot more fat than pork, so those cans become the legs on our couch. The cereal was labeled in the same way. Our boxes said Corn Flakes, and Toasted Oats and that was all. Peanut butter came in one of the big white cans. It too, had a layer of oil on the top that had to be scraped off before you got to the peanut butter.

I will swear to this day that that was the thickest peanut butter ever made. A good friend of mine used to refer to it as "Choke Butter". The monthly visit from the welfare worker was a real thing as well. My mom hid her Tv and what little jewelry she had when the white lady came, just as Diane Carol did in the movie "Claudine". We were so poor that we created a running joke that we were "Po". We couldn't afford the second O and the R needed to qualify us as poor. One of the kids from the neighbor once put a five-pound bag of rice on the front porch as a gag and watched as mom came out and took it in the house. Mom always laughed about it and said it was a blessing. I would be teased about this to no end by the neighborhood kids. Still, inside our house was a happy place. There was none of the tension that we had become use to in Omaha because Dad was not living with us. Then one night he showed up.

The American

I walked into the house, just arriving home from school and dad was sitting on the couch playing with the William, and Tracy who were ages four and two. Mom was in the kitchen cooking, Pam and June were sitting on the floor in front of the TV. I didn't really know what to expect, so after speaking to dad I sat down next to Pam and June and watched TV.

Later that evening after dinner dad called me over and began telling me how I was now going to be the man of the house. As he asked me was I ready to be a man, he began punching me in the chest. The punches were play punches but as they continued, they began to feel less and less so. It went like; "You ready to be a man son" punch. "You ready to be a man son" then another punch that was a little harder. Amos! Mom called to him from her bedroom. Dad let me go and went into her room, where she told him it was time for him to go. There were a few harsh words that passed between them before he left her room. He walked by us on his way out of the door. As he passed by us, we began clapping and shouting YAY, as he left. I would often wonder in later years how much we had hurt Dad that day.

I was now a fifth grader and walked the mile or so to Justin Study Elementary School. I had some problems early in

Anthony Belcher

the year because I had to run home from school and back during our thirty-minute lunch break because I didn't have the thirty-five cents to pay for a school lunch. Usually there was bread and the ever present "Choke Butter" at the house which I use to make a sandwich. On the bad days I would make Cinnamon toast, or sugar sandwiches. Needless to say, I was late getting back to school on most days. When my teacher asked why I was late, I told her the truth.

To my surprise the very next day I had a job working in the cafeteria. This was the same teacher who later that winter noticed that I didn't have much of a winter coat. One day when I came in, she handed me a brand-new fur lined mid waist corduroy coat. Her name has since gone to that place in my memory cells that I can no longer access. However, I hope that she would know that her act of kindness on that day was not taken for granted and would be remembered fifty-three years later. I am sure that this teacher did this type of thing for students before I arrived at Study as well as students who came after I left Study. These are the kinds of concerns and kind acts that teachers due for their students historically and I am sure teachers do to this day. (Coincidently during this current pandemic many parents are learning what the world would be like without schools and teachers.) I hope

The American

this experience will highlight to parents in particular, that we, as a society need to appreciate our teachers more, respect our teachers more, and certainly pay our teachers more.

It was during this time in my life that I feel in love with the school library. Me, Pam, and Amos had always enjoyed reading. Back in the day when mom and dad were still together and could afford regular cereal, we would append our breakfast time joking over would get to read the back of the cereal box. One of the advertising tactics for cereal companies in the early sixties were to add cartoons on the back of the box to attract kids. One of the pieces of furniture that got left in Omaha was a bookcase that dad had made out of an old "Philco" TV cabinet. Once finished he filled it with a collection of encyclopedias, all the works of Robert Louis Stevenson, "Treasure Island" was my favorite, along with other books that I cannot remember.

During our first year in Westfield Pam brought a book home she had checked out from the school library who's title I cannot really remember, however I do remember that it was a book of "Old Negro Folk Tales". The story/fable that was the family favorite was "How the Rattle Snake got His Rattles". We found these stories to be very entertaining and Mom, Pam, June,

Anthony Belcher

and I all read it and talked about how funny the stories were and enjoyed them all. In school I went to the library almost every day. Biographies became my favorite types of stories. I would end up reading the biographies of presidents Washington, Lincoln, Jackson, and Roosevelt, to name a few. Ironically enough, given what I know now about his position on race, Andrew Jacksons biography was my favorite. I shared the feelings of anxiety as "Autie" and the brave men of the 7th Calvary fought and died valiantly, as they tried to make it to the "Little Big Horn" river. I walked to the OK Corral with Wyatt and Doc Holiday to face down the Clantons. I was out in the wide-open prairies with "Bill Cody", and "Kit Carson". Of course, there were the two standard biographies about Negro Americans, Booker T Washington, and George Washington Carver. I loved these stories and their general theme that hard work, honest living and fair play was how you made it in America. Those books gave me hope. They made me feel that maybe I wasn't bad and could be and do good. After all I was an American just like them. Finding out that many in America didn't necessarily see me as one of them would deliver a devastating blow to my psyche and play a major role in the pessimistic and defeatist attitude that would shape my belief system in the coming years.

The American

I assume my parents talked amongst themselves about the politics of the day. I am certain my parents did not discuss politics with their children. In April of 1968, the day MLK was assassinated, we were sent home from school early. On the bus ride home, a little white girl named Becky was complaining in general about why we had to leave school and stated "I don't know why we gotta leave school just because some nigger got killed" I was sitting next to her and upon hearing what she said I slapped her hard across the face. I did not then, and cannot now explain why her words caused such a violent response from me. Maybe, I hit her because she used the word nigger, but I am not sure because usually I engaged in a verbal build up before becoming physical. My response to her was immediate with no forethought and the anger I felt at that moment was all consuming. I was taken aback by how I felt because the simple fact is I had no idea who Martin Luther King was at that moment on that day.

Up to this time I had no real feeling about race. When I lived in England, as I said I was referred to as the little American boy. That the people in England were white, made perfect sense to me in my mind because they were English and that's where white people came from. When we moved back to the states, we moved into a middle-class black neighborhood made up of

Anthony Belcher

two parent households, manicured lawns with domestic cars parked in the driveway. In many black families of that time the word "Nigger" was a bad word and a kid using it would result in immediate retribution in the form of a slap across the mouth. Up to that point in my life I had no reason to think that white people were better than me because they were white. That all would change for me as during the following weeks and days after Dr. King's assassination, his career as the civil rights leader was played out on TV. It would be during this period that I would see the vicious attacks by Birmingham Police and their trained attack dogs on innocent black folk and their kids. I was introduced to the injustices committed on the march to Selma. The scenes of the crowds of white people screaming terrible things at black people because they wanted to go to school, or sit where they wanted on the bus, are burned into my memory.

How could my America treat other Americans who looked like me in such a horrible way simply because they looked like me. In watching all of it unfold on TV every day for the week or so leading up to Dr. Kings funeral I was devastated. Everything I had ever read in all of the biographies about America's heroes, and America's values was a lie. I realized at the young age of eleven, that America didn't consider me worthy to live in the

THE AMERICAN

land of milk and honey. The assassination of MLK and the stark images of White police officers with billy clubs and their German Shepard dogs attacking unarmed peaceful Black folk sent a clear message to me that I was nothing like the heroes whose biographies I had read in 6th grade. It didn't matter how honest I was, how hard I worked, or how fair I played the game of life, I was not an American endowed with the inalienable rights of life liberty and the pursuit of happiness. I was a nigger. For about two weeks I watched the dogs, and the fire hoses, and the police and their billy clubs attack innocent Black folks who were peacefully protesting to gain the rights which all of my schoolbooks, all of the stories I found in my beloved school library said were already theirs because they were Americans. My heart broke and all my dreams seemed to be unattainable. I am pretty sure I have been pissed off at white people ever since.

Two months after the MLK was assassinated, Bobby Kennedy was assassinated in Los Angeles after winning the California primary while running for president. The year had begun with the TET offensive in Viet Nam. Throughout the ordeal the major TV networks Evening News shows broadcast live footage of the Viet Cong storming the US embassy in Saigon around the world. Proving the narrative that what President Johnson and

Anthony Belcher

his generals had been telling the public about having the War under control was false. Americans would never view the federal government with the blind faith of the generation that had come before them again.

That summer Sheila and Cindy came to visit. I remember how happy we all were cramped up in that little two-bedroom apartment. Mom and her seven kids. The girls slept in mom's room, and she slept most nights on the couch. As cramped as it had to be, I do not remember feeling that way at all. The highlight of the summer for us was a camping trip sponsored by the Y. Me, Pam and Bug would be going to stay a week at Chain O Lakes state park. We didn't have a washer and dryer at the time. Mom had not gone to the laundry matt and the day before the trip we didn't have any clean clothes. As coincidence would have it Dad showed up that day pretty drunk looking for mom. He passed out in the driveway in the backseat of my uncle's car waiting to catch mom when she came home. As the day went on me, Pam and Bug were beginning to panic because we knew that Mom may not get home from Foxes bar in time, or in any shape to get the laundry done so we would have clothes to take on the camping trip. Sheila and Cindy were fifteen and sixteen at the time and I am told Cindy came up with the idea to check Dad's pockets to

The American

see if he had enough money to at least get the laundry done. They hit the jackpot and found not only enough money to take a cab to the laundry matt and do all of the laundry, but there was also enough to give us each a few dollars to take with us. Big sisters to the rescue again.

My desire to pester Sheila had not diminished much in the four years since I had seen her, and her finally losing patience and kicking my butt had not changed either. We never mentioned how they had left Omaha. In looking back at that time now, the only thing that seemed to matter was that we were all together. Sheila would get married a couple of years later and move to Flint Michigan where she and her husband would drive to Ft. Wayne regularly to visit on holidays and summer trips back to West Virginia. Cindy would live with us for about a year after she graduated from high school, during which time she gave birth to our first niece and Moms first grandchild, a bright-eyed baby girl she named Tamika.

Dad and Mom were really breaking up. Dad would still show up at all times of the night and day. There were many summer nights those first couple of years where he would show up late, call me outside and talk to me about how much he loved me and

Anthony Belcher

my mother. I was the oldest he would tell me, and I needed to know what was going on. I am pretty sure today that these were Dad's first attempts to tell me that I wasn't his son. He would show up shit faced drunk, and would keep repeating my name "Tone Tone, Tone Tone, I love your momma Tone Tone". This would go on until I could convince him that I needed to go in the house, and he needed to get home. Another night we were playing hide and go seek and I tripped over something as I ran around the side of one of the buildings. I wasn't hurt. I pulled myself to my feet then turned to look for what I had tripped over and there was a body lying face down in a pile of leaves. I started calling out to the other kids, at least five or six besides me, "Hey Ya'll There's a dead man over here." I repeated it a couple of times until all of the other kids joined me, and we gathered around the body lying face down in a pile of leaves. A couple of the older kids grabbed him by his shoulder and began to role him over. They had got him about halfway over when recognition and terror hit me in the gut simultaneously. I started to back away from the crowd, and ease into the house, when one of the kids yelled out "Hey Tony, It's Yo Daddy". To add to my embarrassment Dad began to come to, and started babbling at me "Tone Tone, help your daddy up boy".

So, I helped him up and led him into the house while all

The American

the other kids laughed and pointed. Dad showing up drunk and embarrassing me became an all too common an occurrence over the next couple of years. One day mom told me to catch the bus over to dad's house because he was going to take me out to buy school clothes. I knew she wouldn't send me if he were drunk, so I jumped on the bus and met dad at the bus stop down the street from his house. He borrowed his brother's car, and we went to Wolf and Dessauer, the major department store in downtown Ft. Wayne. He brought me shoes, couple of shirts and a couple pair of pants. We walked across the street and had an Azar's Big Boy sandwich and a chocolate malt. After our shopping trip we went to visit some of my cousins and then went back to the house where he was staying. I remember dad having a few drinks during our visits, but he seemed to be okay. We both lay down on the bed and fell asleep watching TV. My uncle was in the process of moving, and the only furniture in the house was a couch and the bed, which dad had set up in the kitchen. Something woke me up in the middle of the night. It was really hot for some reason. I could see dad standing at the kitchen sink getting what I thought was a glass of water, but he looked funny. He seemed to be all shivery and red. I thought that I was having a dream that had started to fade away before realizing that I had was fully awake and the

Anthony Belcher

bed was on fire, and I was looking at dad through the flames. I rolled out on the other side just as he threw the pot of water onto the flames dousing them and putting them out. He repeated this process then drug the mattress out to the back yard. As I write this now, I believe that dad was in a black out during this whole time. It was like he didn't even see me as he put out the fire and dragged the mattress out of the house.

Luckily, I was not burned and once the fire was out, I just went over to the couch and went back to sleep. I don't remember feeling overly disappointed about how the day had turned out. Neither was I angry at Dad. However, I do remember wondering why dad would go to the sink to get water to put out the fire before getting me out of the bed and away from the flames to make sure I was safe.

I think that my overall feeling was happiness, and relief that I would have new clothes to start the Seventh grade. The year before Mom was not working and could not afford to buy us new clothes for school, and of course on the first day of Sixth grade one of the kids was happy to point out that I was wearing the same clothes I had been wearing the year before. This year it would be different, thanks to Dad.

The American

Mom would start working during my seventh-grade year at St. Joseph's Hospital as a "Nursing Assistant" and would stay there until she retired some thirty years later as a Unit Secretary. Materially, our lives would get better as she was able to buy new furniture, allowing us to finally throw away the potted pork cans that held up most of the old furniture. We would have brand named food in the refrigerator and in the pantry. Still, with five growing kids to feed and clothe there were plenty of weeks when she barely made enough to pay bills. One day I happened upon her sitting at the kitchen table crying while smoking a cigarette and having a beer. I asked her what was wrong, and she said nothing and shoed me away. Mom would tell me in later years what was going on with her that day. She told me that after paying bills all she had left was enough money to buy a pack of cigarettes and a beer. It was payday and she was broke already. She sat there in tears as she contemplated how she would make it through the coming week until her next payday.

One thing about growing up in poor neighborhoods that I believe is universal and exists regardless of race or geographical location is that women in these neighborhoods are always there for each other. Mom had a couple girlfriends, along with dad's two sisters, whom she remains close to even to this day, who were

Anthony Belcher

always around to help each other out during rough times. They would pitch in, one with a bag of beans, another would come up with a chicken, the other adding a bag of potatoes and vegetables. Together they would make a meal for all of us kids. We kids, mostly cousins, loved it because it gave us the opportunity to hang out together. And of course, there was a case of beer or two for them. Somebody would bring some records, we had a second-hand portable record player, and as Marvin Gaye, Gladys Night and the Pips, Aretha Franklin, Rufus Thomas along with all of the great R&B singers from the sixties and seventies serenaded them, these working mothers would feed their kids, complain about how sorry men were, reminisce about times gone by and talk optimistically about what promise the future held, if not for them, for their kids. These gatherings were filled with laughter and love. They serve in my memory as I imagine they do in all kids who grew up in these types of situations as some of the best times of being young.

My attitude and behavior had begun to change drastically during the summer between 6th and 7th grades. I was twelve now and had come to the conclusion that most adults were full of shit in general, and my parents were the worst of the bunch. I saw life in absolutes. You were either right, or you were wrong. You

The American

either told the truth or you lied. No grey area. I was angry at, and distrustful of, any and all authority. I began to give mom serious back talk, usually continuing until I got popped upside the head, at which time I would then walk away mumbling under my breath. To my younger siblings I had adopted the role of tormentor and protector depending on the circumstances. The feelings that I was bad, and unworthy of any real praise or love only intensified, and every negative thing that happened to me happened because I was bad, or unworthy.

The Ft. Wayne community school system employed at that time an educational system which separated students by supposed intelligence, or aptitude in their Jr high, (now middle) schools. The LANE system as it was referred to use the letters X, Y, and Z to identify learning tracks or lanes. The smartest or kids with the highest aptitude were placed in X LANE. Kids with above average aptitude were placed in Y LANE. While kids with average, or below average aptitude were placed in Z LANE. I would be classified as having above average aptitude and placed in Y LANE. With the exception of one or two, there was never more than three black kids in any of my classes and in most of them I was the only black kid in the class. I really didn't have any real discomfort about being in a class full of whites. I had, after

Anthony Belcher

all started school in an all-white country. However, there was a different feeling when I began my seventh-grade year at Portage.

It would be during that year that I heard for the first time a white kid told me that I should go back to Africa where I came from. I think I responded that I came from South Dakota. My interactions with girls were really different. These were the early days of Puberty, and I was seeing girls in a whole different way than I ever had before. I and some other boys had gotten to clowning around and would pull up the dresses of a couple of the girls in our class. It is the kind of punk thing that 12-year-old boys do to get the attention of 12-year-old girls. Especially those of us who weren't part of the "cute" boys that the girls fawned over we had to settle for finding ways to irritate them. I was that kind of kid. These particular girls happened to be white as were almost all of the girls in my classes.

I am pretty sure one or more of the girls reported our behavior to their parents and one of them reported it to the school. One day I got called to the office to see the Assistant Principle. When I got into his office, he told me he had received reports about me and a certain group of girls. He asked me if I knew the girls and I answered that I did and told him they were in

THE AMERICAN

my classes. He then asked did I like the girls he had named and again I answered yes. Then he asked me did I want to, "F" them. I stood there looking confused for a moment and then answered, "fight them?" no. He said no I mean the other "F". I looked at him for a minute with more confusion until I finally understood what he was trying to say and responded "Nooooo".

I think he believed me. He ended the conversation with a stern reminder that that type of behavior was wrong and no little girl would find humor in having their dress pulled up. He then said that I needed to stop it immediately. That was it. I was sent back to class. I don't know if the other boys were called into the office, and I didn't feel like I was being singled out because I was black. I was the instigator of these shenanigans, and the other boys were just following my lead. Preteen boys pulling up girl's dresses and the like as a goof were common occurrences in the popular kids TV shows and movies of the day. As for my sexual prowess at twelve, it was still more wish than reality.

My first sexual encounter had happened back in Omaha. One of the families my parents had known while we were stationed in England showed up for a visit with their daughter who was about four years older than me. During the night after the

Anthony Belcher

other kids had fallen asleep, and the grownups were downstairs playing cards and drinking, the young lady woke me up and took me into the closet and asked if I wanted to do "the nasty". My friends and I had had some conversations about "the nasty" but none of us was quite sure what exactly it was. We knew that it was something that grown up girls and boys did with their clothes off, but that was about it. She pulled my underwear down and did the same with her panties then she took my little "pee pee" which was accommodatingly stiff, and rubbed it up against her "wa wa" we breathed hard, and I think tried to kiss, which was awkward because she was much taller than me, for about five minutes we carried on before we each let out a big sigh, then went back to bed. I thought it weird that the Assistant Principle thought I wanted to have sex with those girls because it was the farthest thing from my mind. I was acting out pranks I had seen in old movies. There was nothing sexual in my intentions at all.

Other than being the class clown, I made both the football and basketball teams that year. Early on in the football season we were practicing after a big rain. It was at the beginning of the year, and we had yet to play our first game. It was one of those practices that midwestern kids love. It was still warm out and the field was muddy and slick. After practice we all started to file

The American

back to the school which was maybe fifty yards from the field. I saw the coach as I was walking his way, standing there talking to someone. There was something familiar about the mannerisms of the man he was talking to. As I got closer that old sickening feeling started to well up in the pit of my stomach. I slowed down and started to veer away from them. I was too late. I heard Dad call my name and I stopped cold in the middle of the field with my helmet in my hand looking at the ground and wanting to be anywhere but there. He was drunk. I could tell by the sound of his voice and the pitying look on the Coach's face. I walked over to them and after a few very uncomfortable and embarrassing moments for me and coach, he was able to get Dad to let me go inside and get changed. I missed a couple of practices after that because I was embarrassed. After our first game I came home in tears because the coach sat me on the bench because I had missed practice.

I never confronted dad during these encounters and there would be others as I grew through my early teens. I was really afraid of him, and more so afraid of my own anger at him and what I might do to him. I felt so bad about how the anger I felt towards dad that one day, while we still lived at my grandparents, after watching an old Spencer Tracy movie where he played a priest. I

Anthony Belcher

came really close to going into a confessional to confess my sins. The Central Catholic High School gym where we would sometimes play ball on Saturday was next to the actual church. I decided against it because I did not know what sin I had committed. This just made me angrier at myself and more fearful of that I anger. I suffered in silence. As I got older, I learned to put on whatever face I needed to address whatever situation I might find myself in. I became a Chameleon. In mental health terminology this is someone who changes their opinions, ideas, or behavior to fit any situation.

Dad did not come around much after that year. The main reason being mom had gotten into another relationship with a man named Roscoe Greene. During the preceding couple of years before Roscoe, Mom had dated a couple of guys, but none had gotten to the level that they were spending the night at our house until Roscoe came around. He was a likeable sort and got along well with all of us kids. He wasn't actually living with us full time during this period, but it was obvious that they were together. Part of Roscoe's likability for me at least, was that he never attempted to be a father figure. He was kind of like a big brother or favorite uncle in that respect. One night we were waken up late by people knocking on the door. Something had happened to Roscoe. He

The American

had been shot. After shuffling us next door to the neighbor's mom went to the hospital. I remember sitting up most of the night just starring at the floor. I didn't really know how to feel about Roscoe, yet I felt like I should feel something. He would survive; however, he would lose his leg. He came back to our house after leaving the hospital for only a short time before being sent to prison for robbing a liquor store.

As I look back on this portion of my childhood, I realize just how young my mother was. If I was twelve, she was just thirty-two. A young vibrant attractive woman, who enjoyed a beer or two and hitting the occasional bar on the weekends. Female headed household were not uncommon in my neighborhood during that time. There would be different boyfriends that came and went, but rarely would they stay around. This was the case with both my dad's sisters and the majority of my mother's friends. As a young man watching these women, I, like most black men today am very appreciative of the obvious sacrifices these young mothers made each and every day to give their children a chance for a better life. However, the lessons many of us don't learn growing up in those households can, in my opinion, all be rolled into one word. Respect. Respect for ourselves, respect for our women, respect for authority. I also believe that the most

Anthony Belcher

important lesson too many Black men who grow up in female headed households do not learn is Responsibility. Responsibility for the women we impregnate and the children we create. That the real measure of a man is how he cares for and raises his family. How he prepares his son for manhood. Instead, we are left with a bunch of fatherless men learning how to be men from fatherless men whose importance/worth to the world is defined by Popular Culture.

"The Moynihan Report", was written in 1965 by Daniel Patrick Moynihan, an American sociologist serving as Assistant Secretary of Labor under President Lyndon B. Johnson His report focused on the deep roots of black poverty in the United States and controversially concluded that the high rate of families headed by single mothers would greatly hinder progress of blacks toward economic and political equality. Moynihan argued that the rise in black single-mother families was caused not by a lack of jobs, but by a destructive vein in ghetto culture, which could be traced to slavery times and the continued discrimination that followed in the American South under Jim Crow. Black sociologist E. Franklin Frazier had introduced that idea in the 1930s, but Moynihan was considered one of the first academics to defy conventional social-science wisdom about the structure of poverty.

THE AMERICAN

Mr. Moynihan's report was attacked by all sides back in the sixties. Not the least for the fact that here was a White man putting out a report about Black people and poverty, which had the audacity to point out the destructive aspects of our culture. As it turns out Mr. Moynihan's report was not based solely in scientific study, instead his keen insight into the destructive culture of the ghetto was learned from firsthand experience while growing up in a pooh Irish American ghetto in Tulsa Oklahoma. In 2016, the US Census Bureau reports that about 70% of all, African American children are raised in single parent female headed households. According to the 2014 U.S. Census Bureau ACS study 27% of all African American men, women and children live below the poverty level compared to just 11% of all Americans. An even higher percentage (38%) of Black children live in poverty compared to 22% of all children in America. According to the U.S. Bureau of Justice Statistics (BJS) in 2013 black males accounted for 37% of the total US male prison population.

When looking at these numbers a realistic argument can be made that Mr. Moynihan's report was prophetic, as much of his report has come to pass.

Thanks to cell phone technology and social media the

Anthony Belcher

microaggressions committed by white people in general towards Black folk and the crimes committed against Black folk by white police officers in particular are posted throughout American and the World. With the George Floyd murder by Minnesota police officers acting as a catalyst we now have young people of all colors, races, genders, religions, and creeds taking to the streets of many of the major cities throughout the world. All coming together in mostly peaceful protests. The courage, and determination of these young people are forcing all of society throughout American and the world to engage in difficult conversations about race, privilege, and policing. I believe that this will eventually lead to significant changes in our laws and collective consciousness. However, Black folk in America achieving accountability for bad cops who kill unarmed Black American citizens and forcing White people of good conscience that as Dr. King said those many years ago, "that Injustice anywhere is a threat to justice everywhere", will have only scratched the surface of the many challenges facing the African American community. Mr. Moynihan and Frazier both in their respective reports point out "a destructive vein in ghetto culture". I believe that this vein in ghetto culture is the last remnants of the forced slave culture of pitting Black folk against Black folk known as "The Willie Lynch Theory".

The American

Willie Lynch gave a speech to an audience on the bank of the James River in Virginia in 1712 regarding control of slaves within the colony. The "Willie Lynch Letter" purports to be a verbatim account of a short speech given by a slave owner, in which he tells other slave masters that he has discovered the "secret" to controlling black slaves is by setting them against one another.

The next challenge for Black Americans is to address the issues surrounding single female headed households which are producing too many men, who do not respect Black women, and too many women who do not trust Black men. I believe Black men raised in single parent households, and in particular, those raised with very little or no relationships with their father's foster long festering resentments towards Black men in general. Groups like "Black Lives Matter" will hopefully strategize ways to bring their message to black communities throughout America where the greatest threat to the lives of young Black men is still to this day other young Black men. If Black women are determined to raise their sons on their own, then we need to address why it seems that so many of the black men raised in female headed households end up in prison instead of college. We all need to understand why it took a White woman to raise the first African American man to be elected president of these United States,

Anthony Belcher

instead of a Black woman. These challenges, not systemic racism, or criminal acts by local police departments, nor the many micro aggressive insults perpetrated against us daily by our White country men and women. It is the disdain and contempt we hold for each other that present the greatest obstacles to the progression of the Black community in America.

There is a line in Spike Lee's new film "Da Five Bloods" where one of the characters says that they were part of a time when a being Brother meant something to Brothers. Becoming a teenager in the early nineteen seventies, I felt the love for being Black. It was real. We Dapped, we greeted each other with "What's happnin" There was love for our sisters, and respect for our mothers. There was honor in being a brother. These are the moral standards that I grew up believing in in the early seventies. However, how I would reconcile those feelings with the feelings of anger, mistrust and self-loathing swirling around in my lower gut would become my greatest challenge

Earlier that Spring, we learned that my Great Grandmother Ross was ailing, and did not have long for this world. Mom, who gives most of the credit of raising her to Grandma Ross, took us all to Mansfield Ohio where we spent most of the summer

THE AMERICAN

until she passed. For most of the time we spent there she was at home. I remember her as being tall and regal in her stature. She spoke quietly, but with an authority earned as the head of her family. She loved the old "I love Lucy" show, which I would put on every morning for her before going outside. To my twelve-year-old self she was both a curiosity and somewhat intimidating. I was confused as to what to call her. Thelma Mae Morris, aka Top, was my grandmother. Dad's mom Grandma Belcher was my other grandmother. It seems silly to me now, but back then what to call her presented me with a real dilemma. I settled on calling her Miss Ross because I thought that addressing her that way was the most respectful. This went on for a few weeks until one day after addressing her that way she called me over, which in itself was shocking because I wasn't sure she knew my name. She said to me in her quiet yet regal and authoritative voice, "Tony, I am your grandmother. If you call me Miss Ross one more time, I am going to give you a whipping." I told Mom about it and her, half-jokingly replied that she may very well get out her strap son you better watch out. Grandma Ross passed toward the end of that summer of 1968 at the age of seventy-eight. I am glad I got to know her.

During the sixties, and late seventies most organized

Anthony Belcher

basketball teams had seemed to have an unspoken rule that there could only be three black players on the team. This structure was prevalent in the NBA, and College Basketball. It was also the case at the High School level and Jr. High School level. The only exceptions to this rule were in cases where the student body was black. Portage Jr. High School was predominately white, and the three black player rules seemed to be in place. I had spent much of the summer before getting better at basketball. When I didn't make the eighth-grade team I felt then, and pretty much feel the same today, that it was because of this rule. I may not have been the best basketball player in the eighth grade; however, I am sure that I was one of the best ten players in my eighth grade and should have made the team. The reason that this is so significant in my life is that getting cut from that team pretty much convinced me that I didn't belong. I would play on the football team in both my ninth and tenth grade years, as a Safety starting a couple games in ninth grade, and as a backup Quarterback on the Sophomore team in Highschool starting one game at that level. I never tried out for the basketball team again, at any level.

My Grandmother, Greg, and Denise had moved to Mansfield about a year before and after my Great Grandmother passed decided to stay. They and some cousins from Mansfield had come

THE AMERICAN

to Ft. Wayne for the weekend. I was thirteen at the time and begged and begged Mom to let me go with them across town to our old neighborhood to hang out. Mom finally relented and off we went. We ended up at the Robinson's house across the street where we all used to live on Cedar Street. Mrs. Robinson was the type of mother who pretty much allowed us kids to drink as long as we did so in the house. That night we wanted to get some drink and play some cards. We put our funds together and she purchased several bottles of "Boones Farm" apple wine for us. Boone's Farm would be the first in a long line of fruit flavored wines, coolers, and other types of alcoholic drinks to come that were targeted toward the teenage market. Many would argue in later years that these types of drinks were specifically targeted toward black teenagers. I don't remember much of what happened after we started drinking that night because it didn't take long before I was in a black out. I woke up the next morning at the bottom of the stairs, my face in a puddle of my own vomit, and my pants full of do-do. My cousins, Greg and Denise were gone. One of the Robinson boys helped me up and into the tub, after which he gave me some clean clothes. When I came down the stairs he too was gone. I was hung over really bad. All I could think of was that I needed to get home and Mom was probably going to be mad.

Anthony Belcher

I started the long three to four-mile walk to my neighborhood feeling about as sick as I could be without dying and had only gotten a couple of blocks before I ran into Dad.

I initially spotted Dad from about a half block away. I could tell that he had been drinking but knew from the way he walked that he hadn't crossed over to the angry place yet. He greeted me like he always did about this time with a "Hey Tone Tone", I know he meant it affectionately, but I hated it non-the-less. He asked what I was doing there, and I made up a story about coming out with Greg and Denise and then getting left behind. I guess it wasn't really a lie, but instead was one of those kinda lies that I imagine most twelve-year-old's get pretty good at. He said that he would get me a cab, but first he wanted to tell me something. Something important he said. Something my mother should have told me long before. We were sitting on the curb at the intersecting corners of Ohio and Lewis Street.

It was a quiet Spring Day, and the weather was about as perfect as it could be. There were very few people on the streets. It was just me and my dad, sitting on the corner having a talk. He with his head bobbing in that bird like way it did when he was drinking, and me sitting there looking at the ground wanting to

THE AMERICAN

be somewhere else. Then he finally said, what I had figured out years before, what he had been hinting at since we moved from Omaha. He said, "I ain't your daddy". There it was, he finally said it out loud. A few minutes passed before I slowly asked, "who is my daddy?". It seemed to me there was a long-drawn-out heavy silence before he responded, "I don't know." That was it. There was no explanation as to how, or why this happened. Just those words. "I ain't your daddy." Nothing else. We sat there for a moment not saying anything. He gave me money for the cab. It wasn't long before the taxi showed up and he put me inside. Still, he said nothing. As the taxi pulled away, I looked out the back window and watched him walk down Lewis Street back the way I had just came from. I don't think I cried, what I remember thinking was I was just disowned by the only father I had ever known.

When I arrived home and walked into the house, I was shocked to find Mom and Aunt Gladys sitting on the couch. Aunt Gladys was all of us kids' favorite aunt. I decided the moment that I saw them that I was going to ask them about what Dad had said to me. I didn't have to bring it up because my mother's "mommy radar" detected that there was something going on with me prompting her to ask me what is the matter? I was really afraid to just come out and ask her who my dad was. Something

Anthony Belcher

instinctual gave me the feeling that type of frontal approach would not be successful. In fact in the short time it took me to answer her, I had already figured out what they were going to say, and it would all center around that dad was drunk and talking out of his mind. The surety of this thought gave me comfort and I told her what had happened with dad. That he had told me that I wasn't his son. I watched their faces closely as they reacted to what I said. Both recovered from the initial shock nicely. Mom was first to respond, and it was as expected, "Aw boy, Amos just drunk and talking crazy. You don't need to worry about nothing he says when he is like that" Aunt Gladys cosigned the "he is just drunk line" and followed it up with "You know who your daddy is". This all was over in a few minutes before they shooed me outside with, going now, go on back outside and play. I did just that, knowing that these two women, whom I respected and loved, and who loved me had just lied to my face.

As I walked over to the park where a group of kids were playing basketball, I felt angry because I was lied to, and angry that they had lied on Dad. I realize now that I was also feeling something else. A feeling that I have to, even to this day fight off. I felt that I was not worthy of the truth, that Dad disowned me because I was bad, that Mom lied to me because I was the cause

THE AMERICAN

of she and dad's fights. When I got to the courts, I called next and watched the current game. It was a sunny summer afternoon in Ft. Wayne Indiana, I was twelve years old, it would be another eight years before I brought up the subject of who my dad was with Mom again.

I made it through the eighth grade that year. I again played football and though I was mostly a backup I did manage to make it into the starting lineup for a couple of games. Sports played a very important role amongst the boys in my neighborhood as I expect it was in all of the neighborhoods across America like mine. If you were good at sports, then you were at the top of the chain in popularity and respect amongst your peers. In the world of teenage males, especially teenage black males growing up in female headed households, sports, or being a musical entertainer was seen as the only viable ways presented to us as a means to be embraced, not only by our community but by America in general. Our only other viable options that we could see were those that were of the streets. There were no positive images presented to the masses to any parts of America of the millions of working class or professional black men that make up the bulk of the black community. For many black folks growing up poor in this country Pop Culture defines who and what they

Anthony Belcher

are. During the time I grew up there was no "Cosby Show", or "A Different World", projecting images of black professionals and college students. With no positive male I like many of the young Black males growing up when I did, looked to sports as the way for me to gain self-esteem and self-worth. I wasn't a bad athlete, and neither was I one of the best in my age group. I did enjoy being part of the football team, but I knew I was a much better basketball player, and believed I had a better than average game. Getting cut from that team broke my heart and killed what little faith I had left believing that I would find success in the school system. From that point on I became a problem student.

Grandma Ross became ill that year and we spent most of the summer in Mansfield Ohio. She passed away late that summer. I remember her as a tall very dignified woman. She was born in the late 1800s, I would have loved to have gotten the opportunity to know her better. After her funeral we went back to Ft. Wayne. I would be starting my ninth-grade year making it my last at Portage before moving on to Elmhurst High School.

The federal bussing mandates had hit Ft. Wayne a few years earlier. I had been bussed out to Abbott Elementary from Harmer Elementary, the year before we moved to Westfield. By the time of

THE AMERICAN

my ninth-grade year it had reached the Jr. and High School levels. The two predominately Black Jr. High Schools were broken up and all of those kids bussed out to predominantly white schools throughout the county. Portage being considered a predominantly white school, black kids from my neighborhood and including the Darling Court kids, made up a very small percentage of the student population. Was one of the schools that would receive new African American students that year. We were all lucky in that Ft. Wayne didn't experience any major race riots, or massive protests like those seen in cities like Boston. There had been a few minor clashes, between black and white students in a few of the schools. If memory serves me North Side High had the worst of these incidents and theirs boiled down to a couple fights between a couple of students. We experienced nothing that would reach the level of what we were seeing in major cities across the country. Along with the busing issues there were still some flare ups between police and young Black folk. It would be just my luck that I got caught up in one such affair after successfully begging Mom to let me go to the local skating rink. Of course, a fight broke out inside the rink and spilled out into the street. A group of duds are throwing fists and bricks at one another with abandon. The skating rink was located on a major thoroughfare

Anthony Belcher

that traversed the city and was used by all. One of the bricks hit a white couple and the police were called and showed up in full riot gear. I managed to get away unscathed making it to my girlfriend's house. I called home and had to listen to Mom's "I told you so" rant, which was laced with more than a few colorful metaphors describing what she should do to my hind parts, before finally having Roscoe come to pick me up.

My overall point is that Ft. Wayne, during my childhood, like all of America was dealing with a transition on how people of color were treated. Though we did have our incidents, overall, the idea of busing, more Black folks, and women being integrated into a what was before a predominately white male factory work force, all these changes were treated with a sort of common sense, and a moral belief in basic fairness. I believe these are principles that are ingrained in all people that grow up in small town Midwest America. To further my point, My cousin Michael Datcher, in his book titled "Raising Fences" recalls a time in his youth where he and a group of other nine-twelve-year old's, were forced to lie on the ground by White Los Angeles Polices officers that found them playing in an empty parking lot with a couple of busted news paper machines. The Police officers went on to treat these children pretty roughly.

The American

In comparison, a little more than ten years earlier, and a few years before my aunt moved the family to LA, Michael's older brother, myself, my brother Amos, and another cousin, were accused of shoplifting in a local grocery store. My two cousins were actually stealing cookies, and a can of sardines. We too, at the time were between the ages of twelve and nine. The police were called. When the White officer arrived, he asked who the two culprits were, with a big smile on his face. He took us down to the station all the while teasing us with stories about this is how "John Dillinger" started. When we arrived at the station, we were allowed to sit at the detective's desk, while we waited for our parents to arrive. As I wright this I realize how much it sounds like a "Mayberry" moment. or we were just lucky we got the "Right" cop. I would disagree, with anything short of that this man was a seasoned Police Officer who had worked with working class and poor families both black and white for years. All he saw were kids, and he treated us like we were kids, knowing that we were much more afraid of what our mothers were going to do to us than we were of him. Which was evidenced when Mom and Aunt Gladys stormed through the doors of the police station. Mom had murder in her eyes, (she hates a thief), and upon seeing her, Amos and I both jumped up with our hands up in the air in

Anthony Belcher

surrender, "IT WASN'T US!!! MA, "WE DIDN'T DO IT!!"

The officer recognizing that Ma had worked herself into a pretty agitated state stepped in to verify that we were not the culprits. The adults began to chuckle when they noticed that Amos and I were still standing with our hands up. After a few minutes of taking care of the official business which amounted to the officer recommended my cousins get a good talking to instead of a good beating. Aunt Gladys promised that they would. Mom replied she recommended the beating. After which they thanked the officer and took us home.

Whereas Michael's experience with White LAPD officers ends with humiliation, my experience with White Police Officers in Ft. Wayne ended with a warm and funny story. I believe that our stories stand as examples of the difference between growing up in the big city and growing up in midsized midwestern towns. I grew up with the horrifying images of dogs attacking black people. I will never forget the shock I felt seeing the twisted faces of White Bostonians spewing out hate filled rhetoric in protest when forced busing hit their community. Like many American black folks, it is baffling to me that The Boston Celtics Basketball team, the first team in the NBA to start five Black players, and the

The American

first to have a black coach could be so loved by the same White Bostonians, who were screaming hate at the black students who were being bussed into their schools. Even today some forty years later you see this duality in White people's treatment and attitudes towards Black people. Even today, some forty years later there are way too many White people with twisted faces spewing hate filled rhetoric. The country I grew up in was filled with daily reports of death in Vietnam, protest riots, and murder. The world I grew up in threaten to burst at the seams as it made the painful metamorphosis toward becoming a "More Perfect Union". Federally mandated busing was happening around the country and in most cases, hate filled protest was its welcome. In Ft. Wayne we accepted it as the new normal and kept on pushing. I am glad I grew up in Ft. Wayne.

My ninth-grade year was good. We went undefeated on the football team, which I believe was a first. Again, I wasn't a full-time starter, but I did play in most of the games if not all as a safety. I would meet my first real girlfriend that year. I would also challenge the record for being late to school. I remember Mom being really excited when I made the transition from elementary school to Jr. High. Now that I was entering High School, her attitude was lukewarm at best, and I asked her why. She looked

Anthony Belcher

at me and with no malice in her voice said, "because I am not sure you are going to make it out of High School son. In all fairness to her, I spent the last two weeks of Jr. High School at home on suspension for getting caught ditching by the Vice Principle no less. The punishment was kinda over the top looking back at it. About six, maybe seven other ninth graders decided to ditch morning classes and go to a nearby park for a pickup game of basketball. Most, if not all of us had already passed the ninth grade and would be moving on to High School anyway, so the punishment was just mean, when you consider that this caused a group of Black ninth graders to be excluded from all of the graduation ceremonies that would be held the last week of school. Did we deserve such a harsh punishment? At the time I really didn't care. By that time, I had fully disengaged from any idea that I was part of the school culture. I went there because I had to. Looking back, it does seem harsh, and I don't believe the same punishment would have been given to a group of White ninth graders. After all, we were only a few blocks away playing basketball.

My overall point is that I was neither hurt nor offended by Mom's observation, regarding my coming future in high school. As it would turn out the ninth grade would be the last full year of

The American

school that I would attend.

Roscoe was released from prison that same summer and moved into the apartment with us. Roscoe was a personable dude who got along well with all of us kids. However, he is also the guy I heard call my mother a bitch on many mornings as she stood in their bedroom door begging him to get up and drive her to work.

It wasn't long before Mom and Roscoe's house sounded a lot like Mom and Dad's house in regard to the drunken fights. I began to realize that my mother due to her own drinking, and underlying issues, started as many fights as Roscoe, or Dad. I have never thought of Mom as a battered woman. Mostly because I was witness to her committing her fair share of the battering. I recall the time in Omaha when she "James Cagney'ed", (mugged for you young folks), Dad with a full plate of spaghetti. She hit him so hard he fell backwards out of his chair, splattering spaghetti sauce all over the refrigerator. All because, as I remember, he didn't step in when Mom's girlfriend's husband slapped her at a barbecue, we were all attending at their house. Then there was the night some ten years or so later that she ambushed Roscoe after he and I had been hanging out. We came in and it was a little late, maybe after midnight. We entered through the back door

Anthony Belcher

passing through the kitchen and her bedroom. As we passed by her bedroom door, she ambushed him, smacking him upside the head with one of a pair of emerald, green cut glass bottles that were about two feet tall, and hefty. We dubbed them the "Genie Bottles", for their resemblance to the bottle from the "I dream of Jeannie Show" She cracked him with a swing that would rival any major league ball player's knocking him immediately to the ground dazed and bleeding. Then she ran to the kitchen grabbed a towel ran back to where he lay moaning, still too dazed to defend himself, hopped over him, fell to her knees, and began to frantically dab at the spilled blood cleaning it off the new rung she had recently purchased.

I helped Roscoe to his feet discouraging his feeble attempts to retaliate, which he was way too dazed to successfully pull off and she still had the Genie bottle. She stood there with it cocked and ready as I was helping him up. As soon as we were past her and into the bathroom, she resumed cleaning up the blood. There are many such stories throughout my pre-adult years. As I retell them now, I find myself smiling, not so much because they are funny "ha ha", but because while drunk people can be scary and mean, they can also do some pretty dumb shit. I would hear stories as well as share my own that very similar to these

The American

in numerous AA, CA, and NA meetings throughout my years of being involved with those groups. They were told with the same humorous feelings that I feel now and when I heard theirs, it helped me to scar over some of my old wounds. They were told by all different types of Americas. Rich, poor, famous, Black, White, Asian, Latino, all of us finding normalcy in the honest sharing of sad tales told by traumatized children living inside adult bodies They were and are the stories of the dysfunctional American family.

I played on the football team my sophomore year. We delivered our high school another losing season maintaining what had become a tradition for the football team. After the season ended, I started to skip/ditch a lot more. Being on the team and having to go to practice, (I learned from my 7th grade experience), was really the only reason I went to school. Outside of football, I didn't really believe school had anything to offer me. I had adapted the "A Black man can't make in the White man's system" attitude and wore it like a badge. However,' I wasn't really a street kid either.

I would spend most of those days watching old movies or the PBS channel. There was a week I remember in particular

Anthony Belcher

where I stayed home because the morning movie was showing a Jerry Lewis marathon and there would be a new movie every morning that week. Choosing not to go to school for me was easy as mom left for work an hour or so before we had to leave for the school bus. I don't think of it now, and surely didn't then, as skipping, or ditching school. I just stopped going. My sister Pam took on the task of waking me and reminding me every morning that I was going to miss the bus no matter how many times I screamed at her to "Get the Fuck Outta My Room"! This became our little routine for about six months before she tired of it. There was one morning this little routine backfired on me. To this day I believe my dear sister set me up as she stood in just inside the bedroom door, in her best annoying sister voice. "Tony you better get your butt up! You gone miss the bus again". I of course respond with my usual "Get the Fuck Outta My Room!" when all of a sudden I hear the way to familiar voice of my mother asking, "What did you just say". Who, unbeknownst to me, did not go to work that day and was instead standing behind Pam, who was by now giggling and saying an innocent good-bye mom on her way out the door. Needless to say, that day I went to school.

One early November evening I got a call from Jackie, my girlfriend. It was pure coincidence that I was at home, and more

The American

so that Mom was also there. I answered the phone and Jackie told me that she was pregnant, and that her mother wanted to talk to me. She put me on with her mom who asked me what I was going to do about this problem.

Once again, there is something about being a mother that gives them this radar like ability to hear things in their children's voices or notice things about their body language that tells them something isn't quite right. Mom's radar must have given her a serious jolt because she walked out and stood in her bedroom door as I continued with my conversation. Jackie's mom, who by now was asking me was I ready to get married and be responsible for the child I had helped to create. I responded like the fifteen-year-old kid that I was with a sheepish "I don't know". She suggested that I needed to come to her house as soon as possible so that we could all sit down and talk. I agreed and then hung up the phone. Once I got off the phone Mom said to me, so is Jackie pregnant? I responded that she was. Mom's response was a little strange to say the least.

Her response was to ask me if Ms. Folks, Jackie's mom, was trying to pressure me into anything. I responded that I didn't know. She then stated that "I will send you to live with your sister

Anthony Belcher

in Flint to live with your sister". She was referring to Sheila and her husband Gary, who had moved to Flint Michigan after they graduated from high school. Mom never asked me if the baby was mine. She didn't yell at me or say anything about how I was too young to be having sex. She didn't say that I was going to have to get a job and take care of my responsibility. Nothing. She put on her coat and headed out the door and across the courtyard to get to the street that led toward Fox's Tavern a few blocks away.

I hitched a ride Cross Town, as we, who lived in Westfield, referred to the Southeastern section of Ft. Wayne where most of the Black population lived. I arrived at Jackie's house and her mother sat us down on the sofa and half joking threatened to give us both a whipping. We all half giggled and then she preceded to have a stern but warm conversation about how serious our little situation was. While I don't remember the exact words that made up this conversation, what I do remember is that I didn't leave there feeling like I had done something bad. Like I was wrong.

This is contributed solely to how Ms. Folks chose to handle the situation. However, as I walked away from their house that night, I didn't have a clue as to what my responsibility to the life I had helped create was. I didn't know how to feel. I didn't know

THE AMERICAN

what to think. I didn't know what to expect. Sadly, I didn't have anyone one in my life who I felt I could talk to about it. Jackie and I would see each other from time to time during her pregnancy and her sister Pat came and picked me up the night our daughter was born. We named her Corvetta, Renee', but it was Ms. Folks pet name for her Peaches, which has stuck to this day.

It was the early 70's and all of the changes that had been fought for during the Sixties were now becoming a reality. My generation would be the first where all African American high school graduates had the opportunity to go to college. Even in the South the State Universities and colleges were admitting Black students in record numbers. I think back to hearing Dad say he couldn't when I asked him why he didn't go to college. A generation later Amos Jr. would accept a full academic scholarship to Purdue University. In towns like Ft. Wayne the factories began to hire Black workers to come in compliance with newly established federal laws. Before then all of the factories were built in or near Black neighborhoods, yet very few Black people worked in those factories. The same was true with the Fast-Food industry. When I lived in Alabama in the mid Nineties Black folks made up most of that work force. In Los Angeles today, the Fast-Food work force is now made up of mostly Hispanics. When I was a teenager in the

Anthony Belcher

70s, Black folks were not hired at these places, as a general rule. This led to the creation of federal job programs that were focused on providing employment to Black Teenagers. It was through one of these programs I got my first job. Mom got a good laugh when I came running to her with my first check almost seething because I wanted to know who FICA was and why they were taking my money. After a good laugh she explained to me that those were the taxes I had to pay to the government. I understood the concept but still didn't appreciate them taking my money. Mom also took me downtown to the bank and showed me how to open a savings account. These are some of the nice moments Mom and I would share during this period in my life.

These were heady times for Black folk across the country. Whenever I hear Black folk say things like the Civil Rights movement didn't change anything, I think this too is part of the "Willie Lynch" theory where Black folks can't see the progress we have made and the obstacles we have overcome because of the contempt we hold for each other. In my day if you were too smart or did too well in school, you risk being classified as a "House Nigga" Don't talk too proper because you sound White. These are all emotional barriers that we, Black folk, have inflicted on each other throughout the years and in some areas right up to this

THE AMERICAN

day. The other phenomenon that I believe comes into play here is how the Black American story has been told to the world by the White American media and entertainment apparatus. Even today in 2020 there are too many Black kids growing up with nothing but negative views about Black history. Way too many of us still fall back on it's the "White Man's" fault.

    Having my own money was nice, but not that big of a deal to me. I never had any high expectations about having material things. I believe part of my attitude was due to my overall feeling that I didn't deserve anything really good. I would get the most pleasure from having my own money when I was able to help Mom out with a bill or buying furniture. Amos Jr., who was the same size as me by then lied about his age and went to work too. We were able to help out in buying new bunk beds for he and William. I was able to buy a twin bed for myself from my buddy Steve who was getting a Waterbed. I do remember getting a whole lot of pleasure from buying my first Maxie coat. The movie the Mack was out, and I had to have a fur collard coat. I couldn't wait for winter to come. In fact, I didn't wait, and one balmy day in mid-October I proudly walk up the street to where all the kids were gathered waiting for the school bus. I got the expected oohs and ahs and nice coats, along with the shit shots about it not being cold enough yet to where the coat.

My other big pleasure from working was that I was able to take Amos and Pam to the Jackson Five concert when they came to town during their "Going Back to Indiana" tour. I went downtown to the local "Eleganza" store, a Black owned business that was based in Chicago and carried all the hippest clothes of the day. I bought with great pleasure a Jimi Hendrix style white puff sleeved shirt, a pair of brown "high" waisted bell bottoms, and matching floppy hat. I completed the look with a pair of brown platform shoes. I Was Sharp! We had seats on the floor of the Coliseum where I ran into an old girlfriend who let me hold her while Michael and brothers did a beautiful rendition of their hit "I'll Be There". Pam and Amos too had a good time and for me it was an opportunity to be the older brother I thought I should be. Instead of the angry bully that I was on most days. These were good times. One Christmas Grandma came to Ft. Wayne at the same time Sheila and Gary her husband was there. We played Pokeno for pennies to well into the wee hours of the morning. These warm family get togethers. These were sober times. As I remember them now, I realize that in most cases Mom's man was not around during these times and her drinking was kept to a minimum. This would change when Roscoe moved in proper, and

The American

Mom's drinking would increase and with drinking came the fights. The fights were for the most part verbal. Amos and I were both young teenage boys by then and Roscoe to his credit never hit her in our presence.

I dealt with these times by staying away from home as much as possible. Mom left for work before I got up in the morning. I made sure I was not there when she arrived home from work in the evening. I spent most of my days watching TV until the kids started to get home from school. I would then leave and go hang out. I would be at the Y or somewhere else in the neighborhood, or I would be across town where I would eventually end up at my girlfriend Cheryl Barnes house. I spent a lot of time at the Barns house during those years. Our families, the kids anyway, had all know each other since we all attended Harmer elementary school.

The school year passed and then did the summer. In the coming fall, I would enter the 11the grade knowing I had not passed the tenth. I had no real feeling about failing in school. I had pretty much accepted that I wasn't going to graduate with my class, and probably wasn't going to finish my junior year. Mom had helped me to get a job in the kitchen of Saint Joseph Hospital.

Anthony Belcher

Being a sixteen-year-old small for his age kid who looked a lot like his mother gained me the heated nickname of Little Cookie while I worked there. It was a nice little job otherwise and I lasted maybe six months before I was asked to apologize to an old white lady, who had called me a little nigger, which I responded to by snatching some trays from her. I had been asking her to push the trays down to me so that I could put them in the washer. She was really slow in getting the trays on the conveyer belt so that they would move down to me to be sprayed and put in the dishwasher. I believe I said something smart assed about how slow she was, and she responded, "You just shut your mouth little nigger"! The next day the manager called me to his office. After listening to my side of the story he informed me that I had to apologize to the old lady before I would be allowed to come back to work. After asking him was she going to apologize to me for calling me a nigger and he is telling me that he didn't thing that was necessary. I declined. I felt that I had not done anything wrong to her and he was not demanding that she apologize to me and that wasn't fair. I can look back at this situation now and find some appreciation for the manager in that at least in his mind he was being more than fair in offering me a way to keep my job. Had I acted in the same manner twenty years prior, the least I could

The American

expect in Indiana would have been to be jailed.

Emmitt Till was beaten and murdered twenty years prior for doing a lot less in Mississippi. I think it important to point out here that there was progress in Americans both black and white attitudes about race. It has taken another forty odd years to bring us to the present where these types of Micro Aggressions are being recognized and properly seen as wrong. For me, that day back in 1973 I walked home feeling bad because I had lost my job and to me that meant I was a failure, while at the same time knowing that I had did the right thing by not apologizing and choosing to leave. When I explained to Mom what had happened, and she did not give me a hard time, I thought that was confirmation that I had made the right choice.

Mom and Roscoe got into one of their big fights, and that proved to be all I could take. I had had enough of their shit! One day while waking home I found a short, handled axe. I took it home and placed it under my mattress with the handle sticking out far enough for me to grip it comfortably. I began to sleep with my hand on the axe. I promised myself that the very next time Roscoe and Mom started that shit. The very next time I was awaken by something crashing against the wall. Well, that would be the last

ANTHONY BELCHER

time they said anything to anyone ever again. Of course, these dark thoughts never manifested into reality. In reality I began to come home later and later.

Cheryl is pregnant. It is early 1974 and I am all but a seventeen-year-old high school dropout. With Peaches approaching one years old, I was one my way to fathering two daughters before I was eighteen. During the last time I put a week or two going to school I would often hear shouts from my friends as I walked through the halls "Hey Tony, how much Pampers cost?), or my all-time favorite "Hey Tony, You baby making motha fucka!". Thus was my claim to fame.

I spent a lot of time hanging out at Cheryl's house. I would develop friendships with each of her brothers and her little sister. After telling her mother she was pregnant the discussion turned to who was going to tell her father. I of course being an honorable man stepped up to the plate and said that it was my responsibility. We set a date for when I would tell him.

Mr. Barnes was a quiet man who went to work every day and came home to his wife and kids. That Sunday night we had all been sitting in the living room watching "Once Upon a Time in The West" with Henry Fonda and Charles Bronson. It is a long movie,

The American

and I was determined to wait until it was over before telling this that I had impregnated his daughter.

Of course, the brothers were all taking turns dropping hints, snickering, and pretty much giving me a hard time throughout the movie. Finally, the movie was over, and I called Mr. Barnes into the kitchen, Cheryl was brave and came and stood near me, not really next to me but near me. So, he walks into the kitchen, the brothers all of sudden get really quiet and they look at me like, "You are really going to do this!"

I stutter the words out to Mr. Barnes, Cheryl is pregnant. You could hear a pin drop. For a few seconds, the world came to a stop. Then he slowly looked at Cheryl and asked "Is that true" she nodded her head yes, he then turned back toward me and looked at the floor for what seemed like forever. He looked up at me and nonchalantly said "Okay, let me go get my shotgun" and walked smooth out of the room leaving all of us stunned.

Needless to say, he didn't come back with the shot gun. Later that week he would sit down with me in his living room and ask me what I had planned to do. I told him that I would go into the service and then Cheryl and I would be married. He said to me that marriage was a big step and asked if I was sure that's

Anthony Belcher

what I wanted to do I told him that it was, and I planned to make a career out of the Air Force. He nodded and told me he thought I had a good plan and he hoped it all worked out for us. He then slipped me a twenty and told me don't tell nobody where I got it from, shook my hand, stood up and walked into his bedroom. It would be the only such "man to man" conversation I would have. It would also turn out to be the last conversation I had with him. My conversation with Mom, would be a lot shorter and a whole lot different.

  I easily passed the test to qualify to join the USAF. I got my swearing in date, and all that was left was for me to get mom to sign the paperwork giving her parental consent for me to join, as I was only seventeen at the time. I came into the house that day, around five pm. Mom was in her usual spot having just gotten home from work. It was a warm sunny spring afternoon. She was sitting in her favorite chair more asleep than awake. I stood in front of her and said Mom, I am not going to school anymore. She looked up and half opened her eyes and replied, "Okay, but you are getting the fuck out of here" She lowered her head and started to go back to sleep. I chuckled before going on to say Mom, I have joined the Air Force and I need you to sign the papers so that I can be sworn in. She is now fully awake and sat up in her

The American

chair. "When did you do this Tony", she asked, I replied that I had first inquired about it a few weeks ago and had passed the test last week. My recruiter would be by tomorrow to with paperwork for you to sign. She looked at me and nodded, her head okay then said "Have him come by here tomorrow around six pm and I will sign. My recruiter came by the next day, we signed all of the necessary documents making me a member of the United States Air Force! Just like my dad.

That day in early May I caught the bus to Indianapolis, where I would be part of an Air Force promotional that was connected to the Indianapolis 500 race that would be held later that month. The gimmick was that 500 young men from Indiana would be sworn into the Air Force all at once in "Monument Circle". Mom, Cheryl, Pam and Tracy and William all went with me to the Greyhound Bus station. I said my goodbye's and got on the bus. I was able to get a window seat and sat waving at my family as the bus backed slowly out into the street. I felt a stab of loneliness hit me right in the gut causing me to lose all interest in the burger and fries we had picked up prior to arriving. I was totally surprised when I noticed that my mother was crying. Here I thought that she would be relieved that I was finally out of the picture. There she was crying the same tears that mothers all over the world shed when

Anthony Belcher

watching one of their children leave home for good.

The storm was raging. After a very bumpy approach we managed to land safely at Lackland AFB sometime in the middle of the night. We were rushed off the plane and ushered onto busses. A short ride later, we arrived at the brand new fifty-man dormitories they had recently finished building for incoming recruits at Lackland AFB. All of a sudden, the double doors of the bus were snatched open and a very pale, small framed but wiry built white man in a very big green "Smokey the Bear" hat with rainwater bouncing off the top and dripping down the side stood there screaming at the top of his lungs. Something to the effect of "Listen to me you sorry sons of maggots. My name is Sr. Master Sgt. Barber!

What followed could have been a scene taken right out of the Stanley Kubrick movie "Full Metal Jacket". The next day we visited the "Green Monster" a complex where you get issued your military gear and go through what looked and felt like the drive thru hair cut line. Remember this was nineteen-seventy-four. Everybody had long hair. Jackson Five sized Afros, along with Mick Jagger like locks were buzzed away with the same cold proficiency. We were then marched over to the clothing complex.

The American

I thought it a good thing we were getting clothing and shoes next because all the marching we had did so far had ruined the platform shoes I wore on the trip. We were then issued uniforms. In the military everything is the same. We were all issued the same fatigues, boots, underwear, t-shirts, and socks. With the evening came chow time. The Air Force, at least at the time I was in was known for having the best meal services of all the different branches of the military. After a hardy meal, we were marched back to the barracks, and it wasn't long after that I and the rest of the fifty brand-new airmen were all fast asleep.

My time in Basic Training was very much like what I had seen on TV. Having spent my early childhood years on Air Force bases I sensed a familiarity about Lackland. The San Antonio heat was stifling hot and muggy. It rained a lot making the tarmac feel like a sauna because of the humidity. The morning drills, which seemed brutal enough were made that much more uncomfortable. There was this particular morning that we were drilling, (marching), after it had rained all night. The asphalt drill pad was hot and sticky from the morning heat and covered with puddles of water from the heavy rain the night before. Hovering over each puddle was a piler of Gnats. Gnats that bite. Sgt. Barber being the asshole that he was found it entertaining to march us

Anthony Belcher

through each tornado like funnel hovering over each puddle on the field. His reasoning was that until we could march through the funnel cloud of biting gnats without anyone slapping at them, we would keep marching through the funnel cloud of biting gnats. I believe it was the fourth or fifth time before we were able to get through the funnel cloud of biting gnats without not one of the fifty of us breaking formation by slapping at said gnats.

Then there was the time old sarge decided that we needed to get to know our gear better. He had us open our foot lockers and wall lockers and instructed us to have a conversation with uniforms, socks, shaving gear and personal things, the importance of being neat clean and orderly. The worst by far was when he marched us at double time for three miles in the blistering heat of the Texas sun. Most of us was wobbly legged by the time we reached the barracks with a couple of us throwing up. Of course, now I understand that even in the Air Force we were a military unit and had to be pushed to the limits of our endurance. You know, just in case. That day, Sgt. Baaber was every low-down son of a bitch and foul filth, foul filth we could come up with. When we were not out training or GI-ing the barracks, we found ways to entertain ourselves.

The American

I, as was my habit found myself entertaining my peer. During the first couple of days on base one of the many places we had to get to was an introductory seminar a sort of welcome to the USAF deal where we sat in an auditorium listening to this really eccentric Colonel explain to us the history of the Air Force going on to further pontificate the importance of and how lucky we were to now be a part of this grand tradition. When I tell you this guy was off the chain, believe me. This guy was off the chain! He was a forty something year old pale individual, a little on the chubby side dressed in his "Dress Blues" He seemed to pattern his look after Douglas MacArthur complete with crumpled hat and sunglasses. He looked a little ridiculous to us, and the golf bag full of clubs he had slung across his shoulder only cemented for us that he was a whack job.

During his hour-long lecture, he would, to put emphasis on whatever point he was trying to get across, line up an imaginary shot, then swing the golf club, making a "clop" sound as if striking a ball, then completing a dramatic follow through, which he would hold for a few moments striking a pose that replicated the logo of the pro-golf tour. He spoke in this stop and go fashion that was both irritating and hilarious at the same time. I had always been pretty good at mimicking people and when we got back to the

Anthony Belcher

barracks, I cracked everybody up imitating the Colonel. Our dorm was set up with two bays, with 25 beds on one side and 25 on the other. I somehow ended up with a copy of the "Happy Hooker". As a goof I started reading the entire book out loud. This quickly became a nightly ritual and I ended up reading the whole book to 25 horny young me. I would read a few chapters every night, then laugh myself to sleep watching the steady line of guys who needed to visit the bathroom stalls.

Overall, Air Force basic training was more like collage compared to the other services. We spent most of our time in classrooms. There were two days spent with the M16, the first day called "Dry Fire", was used to familiarize the troops with the weapon. We spent the entire day learning to break down the M16 semi-automatic rifle, clean it and put it back together. The second day called "Wet Fire" was where we actually went to the range and fired the weapon. I did not do very well, with the M16, in fact, I may have had the worst score in the platoon that day if not in the history of the Air Force. The obstacle course consisted of us crawling through and under a chicken wire fence with explosives going off on each side of you. This all took place during a one-week period toward the end of my six weeks at Lackland. Because I failed an inspection, I think a pair of my shoes didn't pass, I was

THE AMERICAN

scratched from the day trip to San Antonio, which was granted to basic trainees as a reward for having completed the training. I spent my last day sitting in the dorm and planning to go home to get married before going on to my next assignment at Lowry AFB near Denver Colorado.

Cheryl and I were married at her older cousin's house. I believe I spent around three hundred bucks for her a ring. It was a small ceremony attended by our parents and siblings, and I believe Mom and Bug showed up for me. We spent our wedding night in a little cheap motel on the East end of town. We were in love. We were seventeen years old. We were expecting our first child. We didn't have a clue as to what we were getting ourselves into.

Two weeks later I boarded a plane for Denver Colorado where I would spend the next six weeks in Tech school. In basic training one of the many forms you fill out is what was then commonly known as a "Dream Sheet". The form asks what your basic skills are, where would you liked to be stationed, and what job would you want. I answered that I wanted to be stationed in Florida and I wanted to learn to be a professional photographer. As I have already stated I was on my way to Denver and had been

Anthony Belcher

designated a "Warehouseman" by the Air Force and was assigned to the Supply Squadron. Supply was one of those squadrons that was dominated by African Americans. It was viewed by many of us as the equivalency of being assigned to the galley on a ship in the Navy and we considered it a prime example of "Institutional racism". I was the same kid who walked in off the streets and passed the entrance examine easily even after "tic tac toing" the last section of the test. So, I surely was smart enough to get into photography school. Maybe? Maybe not? Would getting into that school have changed how I felt about myself and the direction my life was going in. Maybe? Maybe not?

In any case, I now own my second Cannon EOS T5 that I love and have in the car with me on most days. I have spent hours taking pictures of the beauty and uniqueness of Los Angeles, it's hills and valleys and her people. I am the official/unofficial photographer at all of our family functions. So, while I can say that the Air Force not putting me in the photography squadron stifled my ambition to become a professional photographer. I cannot say with good faith that had I been allowed to pursue this ambition at that time in my life that my life would have taken a different direction than it did. It is what it is, I guess.

The American

I couldn't have been at Lowry Air Force Base for more than a week or two before I got "chose" by this young female airman. I was walking between the barracks and this cute petite brunette stopped me and asked me what my name was. That led to a beer at the Airmen's Club. It was the early seventies and free love, and women's rights were real. We spent an afternoon laughing, talking, and exploring the city by bus. As evening approached, she suggested we get a motel room. I had been married all of two weeks and was already committed adultery. My fooling around would become a common thing during my first marriage. In my mind, as long as I was a good provider, bills got paid, kids got fed and clothed, I did my part. I really didn't see it as cheating at the time and wouldn't fully understand the deep hurt and pain I caused my first wife until many years later. However, as a soon to be sixty-four-year-old dude it's a pretty cool memory.

Some guys and I pitched in together and rented a car and went to see the group War in concert. Again, this was the early Seventies and weed was everywhere. It was theater seating, and I was lucky enough to be sitting in the middle. Folks was lighting up joints at both ends of the isles and passing them toward the middle. There were so many that all you had time to do was hit it and pass it, or as in my case hit and pass one, stick one in my

Anthony Belcher

pocket. By the end of the night, I had a nice supply of joints to take with me back to the barracks. Outside of these stand out memories Tech school was pretty tame. Me and a couple of other guys hung out together outside the Air Man's club. None of us old enough to order drinks as Colorado was a state where you had to be twenty-one. I believe I was the youngest at Seventeen, and the others ranging between eighteen and twenty. We would get an older guy to get us some beer or we would get a half gallon of "Wild Irish Rose" wine, affectionately known as "Skonion" to split between the four of us. It was during this time we shared our views of the world. Watergate, Vietnam, the "Movement" all were happening at that time. We spent many hours in heated discussions about "if the President could be a crook"," what we would do if we got sent to Nam" which though wasn't likely due to Nixon's plan to decrease America's involvement in the war but was still a possibility. We discussed our futures as Black men in America. We recognized that there were plenty more opportunities for us than what was available to our fathers when they were our age. We all expected to either make a career out of the Air Force or go to school which would be paid by the Air Force or get a job at one of the many factories in America and use our GI bill to buy a house. I assume our conversations were no different than the

The American

white dudes at the table across from us in the club. I also assume that they, like us after the "Rose" had made two to three rounds through the group that the conversation inevitable turned to the opposite sex.

I left Denver headed for my permanent station which would be Norton AFB near downtown San Bernardino California, just seventy miles north of Los Angeles. I was assigned to the Supply Squadron as a certified Warehouseman.

Though this was not the Photography job I had hoped for the organizational skills I learned while at Lowry would serve me well throughout the rest of my working life.

Los Angeles in 1974 was to me a beautiful example of black culture during that time in American history. Everywhere I went I was met with positive images of peace, love. soul, and black power presenting an African American landscape that I had only seen in the movies of that time. I, being a teenager who grew up on "Black Exploitation" movies, it thrilled me to no end to be driving through the same streets that "Coffey" Slaughter" and "Foxy Brown" battled to victory over "The Man", the Pimps and the Dope Peddlers that plagued the Black communities of the 1970's.

During my two years station at Norton, I would spend more

Anthony Belcher

than a few weekends in Los Angeles. My parents' good friends and our next-door neighbors when we lived in Omaha now lived in Los Angeles. William Horton was now an Air Force Recruiter. He picked me up after my first week at Norton to visit his family over the weekend. I hadn't seen him since I was about ten and we had a nice talk on the way to Gardena from San Bernardino which is about an hour and half ride. He told me that he was proud of me that I had followed he and Dad into the Air Force. He knew what shape Dad was in and avoided any real conversation about his state of being. Hearing that he was proud of me made me feel good. It wasn't something being said to me a lot in those days. We had a nice ride in his 1973 98 Oldsmobile, painted black with black interior. How I loved that car! He Joyce Toto, Billy and baby Nikki lived in Gardena. It had been close to ten years since I had seen them all and Billy and Tote were as big as me and entering High School. We had a good time reminiscing about the days in Omaha when we were all little kids. William would later take me to see my first professional football game. We saw the Rams and the Detroit Lions. My friend Earl and I got way too drunk and loaded and I for one, don't remember much of the game. Still, it was a big deal to me, and I am forever grateful to William for taking me.

Most of my visits to LA were made to see and hang out

The American

with my uncle Bobby Ross. I had gotten to know Bobby Ross a few years before when he passed through Ft. Wayne and stayed with us for a couple of months. Bobby Ross was hip and a natural comedian. There would be many weekends spent smoking bud and philosophizing about the state of the Black Man and the world in general.

San Bernardino California is the largest city in the county of San Bernardino. Back in the early seventies a big part of the city's economy was built around the base and its personnel. Norton was a Military Airlift Command, (MAC) base and home to the C141 Starlifter, an aircraft designed to move massive amounts of cargo and or troops. My first job at Norton was as a Pickup and Delivery driver. I moved parts from the warehouse to the flight line. I loved watching the aircraft take off and land. The C141 was amazing to watch, however the C5 Galaxy was unbelievable. At the time, the C5 held the title of being the largest aircraft in the world, in comparison the C141 could transport a couple of tanks and a couple of hundred troops. The C5 could transport a couple of C141s! I was completely astonished every time I had the pleasure of watching one take off.

Once you get to your permanent station in the Air Force it

Anthony Belcher

became more like a regular job than what I have heard about the fighting units. My being newly married, I went about the business of buying a car and getting an apartment to make way for my wife and new baby daughter Tonisha.

I found a one-bedroom furnished apartment near downtown and not far from the base. I had gone to LA and with Uncle Bobby as my support I brought a metal flaked blue 1966 Chevy Impala. I felt all grown up the first time I went out and brought sheets, towels, dishes, pots, and pans. I had everything with me on the day I moved in. After washing all of my brand-new dishes I accidently knocked the dish rack off the counter and broke every last dish. I went out and brought more. I stayed in the apartment for about four months before Cheryl and Tonisha would join me. I decorated the place in typical early bachelor pad fashion. With a gold Buddha statue that doubled as an incense burner. My walls were decorated with the center view of the Ohio Players albums, "Skin Tight", "Fire" and "Honey", joined by a black light poster to complete the look. My apartment smelled like incense and weed. I eventually was able to get some dishes into the place that I didn't break and flew my young wife and baby daughter to California where we were going to be a family. We lasted less than six months before Cheryl packed up and went

The American

back to Ft. Wayne. This pretty much set up the pattern for how our marriage would go. Even though we were legally married for five years I don't believe we lived in the same house together for a complete year during the entire marriage.

Once assigned to a permanent base, life in the Air Force, at least then, wasn't much different than life as a civilian. You go to work five days a week and go home. Before Cheryl and Tonisha arrived, I spent as much time hanging out with the fellas shooting dice, playing cards, and getting high. As a pickup and delivery driver I was mobile, and it wasn't uncommon to find me in the barracks watching a sporting event or gambling with my radio sitting next to me during working hours. There is one particular Saturday that comes to mind, where I was working the flight line. It was one of those picture perfect beautiful Southern California days. From the flight line at Norton, you could see the mountains surrounding San Bernardino as clear as day. I was cool with the crew chiefs. The Crew Chief was the enlisted man who ran the crew assigned to keep that particular aircraft in flying condition. Sarge invited me aboard and we took a seat. He in the pilot's chair and I in the copilots. We discussed the difficulty of flying the plane, he promised me that taking off was easy, but it was the landing part that was really hard. We sat there that afternoon admiring

Anthony Belcher

that beautiful view which was even that much more special when you are admiring it while smoking some boss "Acapulco Gold"

I would spend the rest of my military career at Norton. A career that would be shortened by two of the four years I signed up for. As it turns out I once again seemed to be the one that paid the ultimate price for doing things everyone else was doing. Of course, in all fairness, one could easily make the argument that I was quite the screw up and got everything I deserved. I supposed it depends on who is telling the story. In this case that would be me. What I remember from those days is that I smoked a lot of weed and broke a lot of they're shit. One particular incident was when I forgot to tie down a load of 4 C141 aircraft tires which tumbled over onto a Sr. Master Sgt's prized 1969 mint conditioned Corvair. There was also the time I drove the ton and a half into the hanger door. Then there was the big one where I punched a White guy in the mouth for calling me a fucking nigger. That cost me a court marshal and a stripe. It wasn't long after that I was offered an Honorable Discharge and told to go home. As I drove off the base for the last time with a couple of buddies in the car with me, I began throwing all of my military gear out of the window. Shouting and yelling, I'm free, I'm free! The whole time I was thinking to myself, damn I have failed again. I hung around

The American

San Bernardino for about a week before catching a flight home to Ft. Wayne.

I was out of the Air Force and back in Ft. Wayne. It was May of 1976 and I had been away from home for exactly two years. My High School class had graduated and gone on to college or landed one of the many factory jobs around town. A few had even followed my lead and joined one of the branches of the military themselves. The big difference in Ft. Wayne was the by 1976 many of the fair employment laws that were enacted in the city were beginning to come to fruition. There was a big push in all the factories to increase the number of African Americans, women, and other minorities employed in their plants. The big prize of all of the factory jobs was getting hired on at International Harvester, a company that built Cabs for Semi trucks and the Scout truck which along with the then AMC Jeep were the predecessors of today's SUV's. I was hired at Harvester and was fired before my 60-day probation.

I had brought home with me from the Air Force my marijuana habit and continued to get high before, and during working hours, and with that my job performance as well as my attendance were less than satisfactory. Of course, there was the

Anthony Belcher

shame that came with losing the best paying factory job in the city, however it wouldn't last long as Ft. Wayne was booming at the time and as the lyric from the Temptations song "Since I lost My Baby" goes, "There was plenty of work and the bosses were paying" I would only be jobless for a few weeks.

I would navigate most of the remainder of the Seventies in this fashion. Getting a job, quitting, or getting fired from a job, only to get another job. Most of the firings were due to tardiness, missed days, and attitude. It would be many years before I realized that it was my general outlook on life that caused me to find myself in these types of situations. I used to have a saying back then that went something like Fuck God, the world and everyone in it! This is a sad mantra for a young man of nineteen, however I had no real faith in the fairness of life in general, and America in particular, and I was convinced that if I was involved somehow things would end up fucked up. A couple of things would happen over the next couple of years that would start me on a very long road to seeing life through different eyes. The first was a 3:00 am phone call from my mom's youngest sister DeNise, the second, a conversation I would have over Irish coffee with my good friend Billy Simmons.

The American

In the summer of 1977, I had been working as an orderly for the VA hospital for close to a year. I almost literally had gotten fired from Harvester on one day and walked into the VA and got hired on the next day. Cheryl had informed me she was pregnant earlier in the year and we were expecting our second child in about two weeks. Cheryl who had learned during her pregnancy with Tonisha, would have to give birth via cesarian section and the date was scheduled for August 18th. It was about two weeks prior to the birth of my son, that I received the phone call from DeNise.

I had been at the VA for almost a year, and it was time for my evaluation which if positive would all but guarantee me lifetime employment with the VA. I had started my time there with my usual pattern of being late or missing days. However, over the six months leading to the evaluation, I had not been late or missed any days. I had become the go to-guy with problem patience because of the relationships I had built with them. I became the guy they depended on to work the flexible schedule to cover when other orderlies called off. I was scheduled to work the day, evening, and graveyard shift all in one week, which I later was told was a violation of employment law. I walked into the evaluation pretty confident about my future there. I had applied

Anthony Belcher

to and been accepted in the next group to be trained to work in the lab. I was not prepared for that early August morning when I was informed that I was being let go because I hadn't passed my probation. I felt that I had developed into a really good employee over the past six months.

Though unemployment benefits were available back then, I always had the attitude that work was too easy to find and paid more than the unemployment benefits. It was only a few days before I was working stocking groceries at one of the local grocery store chains. Cheryl and I were not actually living together, but I had begun to spend most nights with her as the time for the baby to come was only two weeks away. It was hot that night and Cheryl and I had had a quiet evening at home with Tonisha watching TV. I had gone to bed about midnight and was sound asleep when the phone rang. I picked it up wondering who the hell was calling at that time of the morning. I picked up the phone and say hello, and what I hear from the other end is DeNise saying "Tony I know who your daddy is". Half asleep and not sure if she was playing a joke, or what, as I could tell she had been drinking and the fact she was calling me at that time of the morning irritated me. I believe I said, "yeah right, I will call you tomorrow" and hung up the phone and went straight back to

The American

sleep.

The subject of who my father was had not been on my mind or come up in any conversation at all since the time Dad told me I wasn't his son on the corner of Ohio and Lewis's streets that day back way back when. That was some eight years or so ago. One of the pleasant surprises I got when I returned to Ft. Wayne is that Dad had sobered up. The years of Alcohol abuse had taken its toll on him though. He was no longer the young handsome guy of my youth who could and often was mistaken for white. Although he could and would still sometime mistaken as white. To me he looked a lot more like "Barney Fife" the character Don Knots played on the "Andy Griffith Show".

I lived with him for a short time after getting home and would work with him on his "hustles" which basically was the handy man jobs for wealthy White Folks. These were for the most part menial chores, like babysitting their dog, keeping up the grounds and fetching things for them. Dad was one of the smartest people I know, and I thought he could do a lot better for himself. I expected him to provide a better life for my younger brother and sister William and Tracy who were both younger than twelve. To say the least, I was very disappointed with what he

Anthony Belcher

chose to do once he sobered up. I had long ago accepted that I would probably never know who my biological father was. Once Dad was sober, the circumstances of my birth never came up again. I would never again hear him say to Mom, "You had a baby on me". I believe that Dad treated me and thought of me as his oldest son until the day he died. Today it saddens me that we would never develop a close father son relationship. At that time, I felt I was a grown man. One with a family of my own. I had moved on from my childhood concerns surrounding the identity of my biological father. All of that changed after that 3:00 am phone call.

    His name was Howard Gaulden. He lived in the apartment buildings that sat across the street from Adams elementary school. His was the apartment that had the little fishing boat parked in the driveway. Cheryl's parents lived literally around the corner from him. I must have walked by his apartment and later driven by one hundred times or more on my way to see Cheryl throughout our high school years. After all the years of wondering about who my father was, all the years of looking into strange men's faces wondering if he could be my dad. All of the years I had spent daydreaming that he was a famous entertainer like my cousin Ronny's dad who had been and early recording artist for Motown. He was right here in Ft. Wayne. He was in the

The American

phone book.

The morning after the call I called DeNise and she gave me Pop's, as I would come to call him, name and told me he was in the phone book. I looked him up and wrote down his number. I didn't call him right away. I don't think I called him that day at all. Instead, I called Mom.

Mom was at work when I called and I think I said something like "Hi Momma, I guess we need to talk", and she replied "I guess we do. We made plans to meet at her place when she got home from work. That was fine with me. Her routine never changed, she got off at three-thirty and would get the bus and be home by a quarter to five. It had been this way for years. I arrived at her place promptly at four-thirty and grabbed a seat at the kitchen table to wait the ten to fifteen minutes before she would walk through the door. Well, pretty soon five o'clock rolled around and then became five-thirty. When I looked up and saw that it was now six in the evening, I figured Mom had stood me up. I really didn't get angry as much as I became determined that I wouldn't be blown off tonight. We were going to have this conversation no matter what. I was going to be sitting right here at this kitchen table when she came in.

Anthony Belcher

Mom finally showed up around seven-thirty. It was obvious she had had a few PBRs, (Pabst Blue Ribbon Beer), but she was not drunk. Looking back, it seems odd to me that I wasn't angry about any of it. Throughout the whole day I had not been angry. I am not sure what I felt at the time. Anger would come later, but that night I just wanted to hear the truth.

I was sitting at the table when she came in. I could tell she was a bit nervous about facing me. After the initial "Hi Ma, Hi Tony, when she walked in the door there was a moment of, not so much an awkward silence as it was sort of mutual time out. It was like we were two people who had been with this elephant in the room and the elephant actually spoke, and we didn't know what to say to each other. That is how I remember it now. What actually happened is that she came in put her beer in the fridge, sat down pop open another can and said "Well you are a patient so-n-so ain't Ya? I smiled and said yeah ma I guess I can be. I then said, "Why didn't you tell me"? She replied, "I would have never told you. I said to her but Ma, you knew what Dad was doing and telling me. You knew. She said, "Amos didn't keep his word." I offered to get an annulment, but he didn't want to. I don't remember this being an emotional conversation. I would say it was subdued, at best. She went on to say that she loved Howard, but he was married.

The American

That was about all the information I would get from her about their relationship. I didn't say much during all of this. I think I had a beer with her and left shortly after that. As I drove over to Cheryl's that night, I was thinking that finally after all this time I am going to meet my father.

While waiting for Mom to get home I had called the number in the phone book next to the name Howard Gaulden. He answered the phone and I said to him "Hello Sir, my name is Tony Belcher, and they tell me you are my father." He replied, "That's what they tell me too." We then made arrangements to meet the next day.

I arrived at his apartment that next evening a little after five. When I walked past the little fishing boat parked in the driveway to his door, I again thought about how many times I had walked past this apartment over the years. I knocked on the door and after a few minutes he opened the door with a hardy "Hey Man! Come on in! Once inside he tried to hug me, but I ducked and stuck out my hand to shake. He chuckled a little and for a moment we stood there looking at each other. He was tall, about six three with a salt and pepper afro and goatee I didn't see an obvious resemblance to him, but I felt there was something familiar about

Anthony Belcher

him. He looked at me and like most folks who knew my mom, said "You look like your Momma! He was wearing an African night shirt that was what the hip brothers wore at the time. Today it is known as being woke.

In short Pops as I would come to call him was Cool. His apartment was small but neat. There was a couch with matching coffee and end tables, a lazy boy type armchair, a small organ and his guitar and amp. The house smelled of fresh coffee and weed. We sat down, he on the couch and me in the lazy boy. We each pulled out a joint to offer the other almost simultaneously. He began the conversation by saying "Hey Man, I am sorry for what we may have done to you. I was married and your mom and I were fooling around, and that fooling around turned into you. When she told me about you, she forbade me to say anything to you about it." As I sat there listening to him, I really didn't know what to make of it all. I believed everything he said.

Mom herself had just told me she never wanted me to know the truth. As I sat there looking at this man who was my father try to see any resemblance between us. He was tall, and I was short. He had a salt and pepper goatee to match his salt and pepper afro. I had yet to grow any facial hair to speak of and

THE AMERICAN

wondered if I would look like him when I grew older. I wasn't sure. However, it was his knees that convinced me that I had finally met my father. When he sat down on the couch to roll a joint, he pulled his robe up exposing his knees. His knees were shaped and looked exactly like my knees. They looked exactly like my daughter Tonisha's knees. I was definitely this man's son!

That first night we would spend a couple of hours sitting there talking about Ft. Wayne and the people we knew. He then took me over to his sister's house Josephine and her husband Frank. I knew their daughter Vivian from around town and may have at one time made a pass at her. Once again, the greeting was warm and very welcoming. My Aunt Josie hugged me and then held me at arms-length while saying "Let me see who you look like" You look just like your Momma! The fact is, back then, I did look just like my mother. We spent a short time there before I headed home. Pops, which I believe I was calling him by the end of the night, told me I that he was happy to meet me and that I was always welcome. As I drove to the house after, I wasn't sure how I felt, however, I was quite sure that I had just met my family.

Over the next few days and months, I would find out that it was who my father was not the secret I thought it to be. It seemed

Anthony Belcher

that all of the adults, my aunts, uncles, and grandparents knew the truth. I felt betrayed by all of the adults in my life. I felt that they had watched me suffer through anguish and pain over this issue and yet all stood by and said nothing to help me understand. They all knew. They all gave me the same bullshit answer when I asked them why none of them told me the truth. They all said it wasn't their place to tell me. While I understand that sentiment now, at the time I was deeply hurt by it. I perceived it as that they all claimed they cared about me yet none of them could see my pain, or worse didn't care enough about it to tell me the truth. I was pissed off about it at the time and it only reaffirmed the unfairness of my situation and my pessimistic few of people, and life in general.

The set of circumstances that aligned and led up to Mom having this conversation with DeNise and Beverly. Was that Beverly, one of my baby sister Tracy's friends, who also lived in the apartment located cattycornered from Mom's place, was Howard Gaulden's brother's youngest daughter, and his niece, making her my first cousin. She had an older brother who's name coincidently was Tony that was about a year younger than me, and he and I regularly hung out together, especially during the times I was staying at Moms, which was quite a bit up until lately. I can

The American

imagine Mom being very nervous at the prospect that Tony and Beverly's Mom had seen me and would tell them who I was, and they would then tell me. Tony and Beverly Gaulden had moved into that apartment maybe a year prior to the secret coming out. It must've been a stressful time for her. Throw in a six pack or two of Pabst Blue Ribbon and the truth did set me free.

    I would become very familiar with Pops little apartment, as I would spend many hours of the next couple of years bonding with him. We would discuss everything from the problems and politics of the day, our respective childhood, our respective times in the Air Force. We were building a father son bond that was free of all of the barriers that are erected between fathers and sons who grow up in the same house together. I was twenty years old, married and the father of three. However, I was a young and very immature twenty in many ways having grown up with no real male influence in my life. I was starving for a father. I needed to feel that I wasn't a mistake and the cause of everything bad that had happened in my life. Pops, too for all of his talk of being okay by himself was as much in need of our relationship as I. The added benefit was the discovery that the more we talked and shared ideas and feelings the more we realized just how much we were alike.

Anthony Belcher

A couple of years after meeting Pops his uncle Harold died and he asked me to go with him to Grambling Louisiana for the funeral. I would meet his father, my grandfather Andrew, as well as his uncles and Aunts. Uncle Harold, who's funeral we were attending had played Negro league baseball. All of the aunts were teachers and social workers. We flew into Atlanta and from there into Monroe Louisiana where I would meet my grandfather Andrew Gaulden for the first time. We got off the plane walking down the stairs, back then they rolled them up to the door of the plane, and I saw this old distinguished looking man dressed, complete with fedora hat and trench coat. He had a leathery face and wise eyes.

I walked directly up to him and stuck out my hand and said "Hello Sir, my name is Tony Belcher, and I am your grandson. He took my hand while looking over my shoulder at Pops who was standing behind me. He then shook my hand once and said, "How do" then to Pops, "Howard, how was the trip". Pops responded, then he grabbed the bag Pops was carrying and said "The car is over here" as he walked past us headed in the direction of the car. I was a little taken aback by his action to my greeting. I wasn't sure if he accepted me or what. After taking a few steps passed us he turned around and looked at me and said "HA" shook his head and

The American

kept walking. We drove to Uncle Franks house. He was a jolly guy who was blind but knew who people were by the rhythm of their walk. He remembered Pops when he came in greeted him with a big hug, and said I hear you brought Little "Happy with you" and so I was dubbed for the rest of the trip. Pops Aunts were all there along with a few cousins. They greeted me with hugs, oohs, aahs, and for the first time in my life I heard someone say to me, wow you look just like your dad.

After the funeral services, the next day I was surprised when Grandpa Andrew walked up to me with a couple of older ladies decked out in their nicest hats and church dresses on each arm and stated with beaming pride, "This is my grandson, Tony". It was a totally unexpected moment, which left me all but speechless. Pops and I spent the night at Grandpa's house, or one of his girlfriends, I seem to remember that he had a little house, not much more than a shack that was out in the woods somewhere, that he only stayed at when he was between girlfriends. That evening we sat in his living room after dinner talking. He pulled out an old guitar and laid it across his lap, then after putting what is called a "slide" over his finger began to pick out an old bluesy riff. Watching him sitting in front of the raging fireplace and occasionally spitting in the fire causing the flames

Anthony Belcher

to hiss, gave me this strange yet warm feeling.

My grandfather was born in either the early nineteen hundred or the late eighteen hundreds, only a generation after slavery. I can imagine that a warm fire, an old guitar, the comfort of a home and a good woman was about as good as it gets to him. I loved him in that moment and was grateful to be in his presence. Pops and I had to share a bed. It was a big king-sized bed that seemed to be about three feet off the floor and covered with homemade quilts that felt like they weighed fifty pounds. We were treated to a breakfast of bacon, eggs, potatoes, grits, orange juice, and fluffy buttery buttermilk biscuits that were as big as baseballs. After breakfast Grandpa drove us to the airport in Monroe. As we said our goodbyes and stood there watching Grandpa walk back to his car, my eyes suddenly filled with tears as it dawned on me that I finally had an identity. My long search was over. I wasn't a mistake. I had just spent the last couple of days with three generations of people who all looked and sounded like me. I belonged. My family were brick masons and educators.

Meeting, and getting to know Pops never caused any real conflict within me as to my identity as Tony Belcher, and how I felt about my Belcher cousins, aunts, and uncles. I felt good that

The American

when I met one of Pops' aunts she said well, Mr. Belcher we just gonna have to change that name to Gaulden like it was supposed to be. The acceptance by the Gaulden family I received while in Grambling had filled a huge hole in my being. For me there would never be an issue about choosing. The Belchers were my family, and as I got to know the Gaulden family, they just became that side of my family. My first cousins, Gilbert, Steve, and Ronnie all have at one time, or another gone with me to Pops apartment. While I had no need to make any announcements to the world about my newfound family, I had no intention of keeping it a secret. The only parent of the now three I could claim that I had no conversation with about the circumstances of my birth was Dad. To this day we have never had an in-depth conversation about it at all.

"I can be as funny as Jimmy Walker" I remember thinking this one evening after watching Good Times on TV. For years people had been telling me that I should go into show business. After meeting Pops, who drove a Truck for a living, but was a jazz musician in his heart, I had made some attempts to play music. At the time I was into the "Funk" music of the day which used the bass guitar as a lead instrument, and I decided I wanted to play bass. While I could figure out the mechanics and learned to play a few songs, it was obvious to me that I didn't possess the God given

Anthony Belcher

talent that Pops, my friend Ron, or my cousin Ronny displayed as soon as they picked up their instruments and began to play. As, my Aunt DeNise put it one day, "Boy you ain't gonna make no money plucking on that thing". Still, I was certain I had talent, though not the musical kind, and had a future in show business. I just had to figure out how I was gonna go about getting into to acting. My good friend Billy Simmons would soon provide me with an answer.

Willie Simmons Jr. was about four years older than me. He came from working class folks, his mom worked as a secretary at Portage Jr. High, and his dad worked at the Harvester as well as had his own plumbing company and did odd plumbing jobs during the weekends. Typical working class America family. I met Billy as we called him, through Steve Ransom who l had become best friends with around the time, I was going to ninth grade. Billy being the only boy in his family sort of adopted a few of us as little brothers. He would eventually become close with all of my siblings, and he was the only person at the time, including my Pops, that I trusted with telling my dreams to. We used to frequent an old part of downtown Ft. Wayne which had a couple of bars that were decorated in the style of the bars of the 30s and 40s. It was sitting in one of these bars that I told Billy that I

The American

was interested in acting. He laughed and said yeah right! It took me a couple of minutes to convince him that I was serious, and that I wanted, and needed his honest opinions on how to go about getting started. Billy said to me, well man there is a local theater right down the street. He said they put on plays all the time, and you should go down there and audition for one, that way you can find out if you have any talent for acting. I looked at him with astonishment. Could it really be that simple, I thought? I had no idea that Ft. Wayne had a theater that put-on plays. The next day Billy came by the house with a book titled Respect for Acting written by Uta Hagen.

The Ft. Wayne Civic Theater had been around since 1927 and had recently moved into the brand-new Performing Arts Center located at 303 East Main Street in 1973. The theater though not famous was ranked as one of the best in regard to production standards and public participation. I knew none of this when I walked into the Youth Theater to audition for my first play. It was the summer of nineteen 80. Cheryl and I had broken up for the last time and I was back at Moms. After the bar conversation with Billy and reading Ms. Hagen's book. I had begun to watch the paper for notification of auditions being held at the Civic. I locked in on one that was being held at the Youth Theater. I noted

Anthony Belcher

the date and time and when it arrived, I showed up not having a clue of what to do next. I was ushered in and was introduced to the director, Harvey Cox, who looked me up and down, then handed me a few pages of script to read. While I was reading, he was sort of paying attention while he simultaneously talked on the phone with someone from costumes. When I finished, he said thanks and told me he would be in touch. I left there thinking well, that's the last I'll hear from him. I was completely surprised when I got home, and Mom told me that some man from the Civic theater called here for you. "He sounds like he's Gay." she says, "What he want with you"? I think I might have told her that I had applied for a job there. I could tell by her tone that she wasn't going to be supportive. I called back and Harvey Cox offered me a small part in his production of the play "Steal Away Home".

I remember Harvey as being a kind and caring person who really loved working with young people on the stage. His rehearsals were serious and at the same time felt light and fun. I was to play a Quaker Preacher who helps two runaway slave boys along the Underground Railroad.

There have been only two occasions in my life where I walked into a situation and where I was totally comfortable and had no

The American

doubts that I could do this. The first time this occurred is when the curtain went up that Saturday afternoon and for the first time in my life I walked out on stage. As I waited for my cue to go on, I had no doubts that I could do this. The show was well received, and Billy and Pops were there for the opening performance.

While my first acting experience could by no means be considered a test of my potential skill level, I only had one very short scene with no more than ten lines. However, there was an occasion where I improvised a prayer to fill in a noticeable silence in my dialogue that worked out perfectly the first time. The second time not so much, but I did learn the value of writing things down, because I had forgot exactly what I had said in the previous performance and stumbled noticeably through it the second time.

There was another occasion where a piece of the set actually came off in my hand. I was able to stay in character and not miss a beat. When the show was over, I was pretty sure that I wanted to be a professional actor. Over the next few months, I auditioned for everything they had. The one I remember most is the audition for "The Best Little Whore House in Texas" I had no more idea of how a musical audition went than I did for any other

Anthony Belcher

type of audition. The only reason I knew the story was that I had seen the movie of the same name, starring Bert Reynolds, and Dolly Parton. Needless to say, I was not prepared, and actually almost didn't go through with it, once I arrived and saw all the other actors who had prepared musical numbers complete with sheet music and a few had their own accompanist. I will say this for myself I was certainly determined which gave me courage.

When I realized what was going on I couldn't for the life of me think of anything to sing. I knew I would have to sing A cappella whatever I sang because I had never sung with a piano player before. Then there was the fact that I in no one's stretch of the imagination had a good singing voice. All of this was flying through my head while I waited my turn. The only song I could think of that I knew from beginning to end was "Take Me Out to The Ballgame". I went with it and gave a very poor rendition of that song. I felt pretty stupid afterwards and had a good laugh at myself. It would be the first time in my life that I didn't do well at something and didn't internalize it as a failure. Somehow, I instinctually understood that if for no other reason than I was going to be remembered for giving the worst audition of the day, I was going to be remembered! Most importantly I felt good that I had gone through the audition.

The American

While having to admit that my audition was not what I wanted it to be, I knew that I could improve, and looked at the whole ordeal as a lesson learned. I was not surprised when I learned that I would not be cast for "The Best Little Whorehouse in Texas," and auditioned for the next production which I believe was "Born Yesterday." These were all auditions for the main theater and were conducted by the Artistic Director Richard Casey. After I read for "Born Yesterday" Dick as I would come to know him pulled me aside and said that he was casting for a play called "A Raisin in The Sun" for a six-week run beginning in October and that I should audition then.

Richard Casey came to the Ft. Wayne Civic Theater from the acclaimed American Academy of Dramatic Arts in New York City, where he had taught acting to the likes of Cleavon Little, Danny DeVito, and Robert Redford. Since taking over the Managing Artistic Directorship he had transformed Ft. Wayne's little theater of fifteen thousand in annual attendance into a venue that saw fifty thousand a year due to the increased professionalism and quality of his productions. Ft. Wayne Civic became the outstanding community theater in all of Indiana and one of the best in the nation. It was the reason that the Ft. Wayne Civic Theater would produce for the very first time, an all-Black play. I have heard

Anthony Belcher

rumors of the resistance Richard had to overcome in getting the governing body to agree to producing its first all-Black play. From what I was told back then the board had concerns about if an all-Black play would make money, and many of them didn't believe that Dick would be able to find enough talent within the F t . Wayne Black community to fill out the cast. Dick offered to bring in a professional actress from New York to play the role of the mother to satisfy their concerns about the box office and assured them he would be able to cast the rest of the roles from the within the Black community. Dick found Ms. Gertrude Jeanette from New York to come in and play the role of the mother and to my surprise, then cast a twenty-three-year-old kid from Westfield in the lead role of Walter Lee Younger. That twenty-three-year-old was me.

Ms. Jeanette was not present for the audition process or the first few weeks of rehearsal. Again, rumor has it that Dick didn't want to bring her in until he was sure he had a cast talented enough to support her. The audition process was a simple reading. I felt good about how I had read and thought I had a good chance of landing the role of Assegai, or maybe George Murchison, but never in my wildest dreams did I expect to be cast as Walter Lee. I guy I knew from high school, Bradford Smith was cast as

The American

Assagai, with Karen Williams as Ruth Younger, Donnette Banks as Beneatha Younger, James Johnson as George Murchison, Sean Rogers as Travis Younger, Joe Abella as Mr. Linder, Steve Wallace as Bobo and Angela Wright as our PA and stand in for Gertrude until she arrived.

After the cast was set, we had our first meeting with Dick. The most interesting memory I have from our first meeting with Dick is that it was the first I had ever heard of "CP Time." He was making it very clear that he would not tolerate any arriving at the last minute or tardiness and that in his world there was no such thing as CP time. I actually had to ask, and I believe it was Karen Williams, what the hell is "CP Time". When she told me it meant "Colored People Time" I was both tickled and a little ticked off that he felt he had to mention it. I am not, in any way suggesting that Dick Casey had committed some unintended racial slight. The fact that all of the other Black people in the room new exactly what he meant when he brought it up is only testimony to how little I knew about somethings that were considered staples of the Black community. I can honestly say that I don't remember ever hearing that phrase being used by any of my family members when I was growing up.

Anthony Belcher

We began rehearsals with Angela standing in as Momma. I knew all of my lines on day one and was able to focus on the blocking of the play. There was a point in the early rehearsal process where Dick was not happy with how I delivered a line. The line is said during Walter Lee's, criticizing of his sister Beneatha's "Black Knee Socks", for reasons I am not sure of today, Dick did not like the way I said Knee Socks and we spent more than a couple of rehearsals going over the line again and again, until in frustration he said that I didn't sound like any of the rest of my stage family. Over the years I have given this some thought and feel that Dick thought I didn't sound "Black enough".

I contribute this more to my having spent part of my developing years as a child in England. Black people throughout my life have said that I didn't talk like a black person. We got past it and I learned as we went on that Dick treated us all as professionals and demanded that we conduct ourselves as such. Still, my old demons of self-doubt had raised its ugly head and the voices were whispering to me that I wasn't good enough. By the time Gertrude arrived and joined us for rehearsals I was afraid that Dick was going to replace me as Walter Lee.

My anxiety about being replaced was just that anxiety, and

THE AMERICAN

nothing more. Still throughout the process of rehearsals, and even with the success of the show I had this foreboding feeling of "waiting for the other shoe to drop", that nothing happening for me that was this good could last. However, I am getting ahead of myself. Gertrude Jeanette was duly impressed with the level of professionalism Dick had installed into our little group when she joined us after two weeks. We rehearsed six nights a week, off only on Sunday. Over the next four weeks we bonded and grew as a cast. Dick pushed me harder, I felt than he did the others, and a couple of times Gertrude came to my rescue by suggesting that we move on in the spirit of continuity.

It would be Gertrude who would be the first to say how much I had grown into the role. In all honesty I didn't really understand what that really meant; however, I was sure that it didn't mean that I "Sucked"! When it came time for opening night, we all felt that we had a good show that people would enjoy. We were not, prepared for what would come next. The show was a huge hit! We were all suddenly stars. All of a sudden, we were being interviewed by local newspapers and invited to speak in elementary schools.

I even got the opportunity to return to Elmhurst High School

Anthony Belcher

where I ran into the eighth-grade teacher who's hand I had rather forcibly removed from my arm back in eighth grade, who now worked in the theater department at Elmhurst. Though she was nice and polite, I couldn't help but enjoy the obvious discomfort she displayed as she sheepishly greeted me with "Tony Belcher I thought you would be in jail. I smiled and replied I guess I fooled you and then she was asked by her boss to go do something else while she introduced us to the students. I could see that she did not appreciate being left behind that way by the look on her face as we walked away.

Sometimes you get a little justice from this world. As word of mouth got around the city about the show our audiences began to be comprised of more of Ft. Wayne's black community. Black audiences are more interactive with the action on the stage and there were a couple of nights I could hear folks cheering Momma along as she beats Walter's back in agony when it is revealed he has lost almost all of the insurance money. The last night of our run people were sitting in the isle and on the stairs. We outsold the Wiz Road show, which opened at the Embassy Theater that night. We were a hit, and I was a local star. I had no idea what I was going to do next.

The American

Only a few weeks would pass before what was going to happen next would be decided for me. I was asked to join Gertrude and Dick at a meeting a couple of days before Gertrude was to leave going back to New York. I had spent the past couple of weeks after the show had closed being introduced to the leaders of the Artistic community in Ft. Wayne. One such meeting was with the then head of the Ft. Wayne Ballet. I remember being really confused when I met the Director and asked him outright why he thought I would be interested in ballet. To my pleasant surprise he said that he was very impressed with how I moved on stage and especially the grace I had shown when I jumped up on the table for Walter Lee's drunken speech. He also informed me that Ballet was certainly not the only form of dance he taught and that he thought I would enjoy learning modern and jazz dancing. He told me to think about it and let him know because he could get me a scholarship. I said I would but to be honest, it all reminded me of the time my football coach asked me to come out for the gymnastic team. Back then I thought dance like gymnastics was let's say not manly enough for me at that time.

I never tried out for the Gymnastics team. As it turned out I would never have to make the decision about enrolling at the Ft. Wayne Ballet. When I arrived at Dicks office that morning

Anthony Belcher

Gertrude and another gentleman whose name I cannot remember but would later learn he was an Executive for the local branch of Pain Webber Jackson and Curtis a major New York City brokerage firm, were all waiting for me. Introductions were made and they began talking about the American Academy of Dramatic Arts, and working at Pain Webber, and would Gertrude be able to put me up for a while. Due to being just a bit hungover, I hadn't really been dialed into the conversation up to that point but perked up after hearing them talk about putting me up a while. Dick had told me at the opening night party that he thought that I could be a professional actor.

We had both had more than a couple of drinks when he said it and I hadn't given it much thought until now. Because the next thing I heard was Dick informing me that he had secured me an Addition at the AADA, and would I like to go live in New York. While I was still trying to absorb this, I heard Mr. Pain Webber Executive say he would help me to get a job at the New York Office, then Gertrude said that she had a spare room that I could use until I got on my feet. I finally said yes, of course, thank you so much all the while grinning from ear to ear. I was going to New York!

The American

The family gave me a big send off at the train station in downtown Ft. Wayne. I was on my way to the big city to become a star! That is what was predicted and that is what everybody believed was my destiny. Me? I wasn't so sure of what was going to happen next. In hindsight I realize that had events played out to where I had gained some training and most importantly some confidence in my ability things might have turned out differently. As it was, I boarded the train that night feeling more like I was running away from something instead of heading into a future where I would finally get the chance to prove my worthiness to the world.

The train ride from Ft. Wayne to New York was about twenty or so hours. I don't remember engaging in daydreams of how I was going to become a star. I don't remember much about the trip at all. I knew I had a job interview at Pain Webber and an audition at AADA all scheduled for my first week there. Gertrude met me at Grand Central Station, and we took a cab uptown. I do remember looking out the window of the cab seeing the city and recognizing places I had only seen in the movies prior to that day. We crossed 110th street and were officially in Harlem. Gertrude lived on 135th and Lennox Ave. Her apartment was located directly across the street from the YMCA, and down the street from both

Anthony Belcher

the Schomburg Library, (now called the "Research Center for Black Culture") and the Harlem hospital.

Gertrude lived in a relatively new building facing 135th street. Monday morning, she showed me how to take the subway downtown. The first time I walked into the tunnel at 135th and Lennox I was shocked by the number of people I saw lined up waiting to get on the train. There were at least three rows of people "Black" people all waiting to get on the train. I was even more shocked when the number three train pulled in and the doors opened, and it looked to me that the train actually sucked in all of the people that were standing in front of me. I actually didn't move for a second until Gertrude started pushing me towards the door saying "you gotta move man" as we hustled into the already full car. In what seemed like a very short time, about twenty-five minutes, we were whisked from 135th St to Wall Street located about ten miles south in lower Manhattan.

While other big cities have rail systems as part of their public transportation apparatus, I would argue that no city's train system is more efficient than New York City's. The speed, if not comfort in which they move masses of people throughout the city is amazing. Gertrude showed me how to get to Pain Webber

The American

then told me where to catch the train back and left me to my own devices. My reaction to being amidst the skyscrapers is best described in the opening of Stevie Wonder's song "Living for The City". The pace of the city was both exhilarating and amazing to watch. These people were going places and had places to go. People of all races all talking and sounding to me like the characters in the "Godfather". I found my way to the offices of Pain Webber Jackson and Curtis. The offices were located at the corner of Broad and Wall streets and was directly across from the New York stock exchange. I made my way to the designated floor and was interviewed by the department manager and told to report to work the following Monday. Again, I thought about having spent the last year in Ft. Wayne looking for a job, and here I was after one day in New York and I working in the financial district. Wow!

    I had been in New York for all of a week when December 8th, 1980, rolled around. Of course, that is the date that Mark David Chapman of Decatur Georgia ended the life of John Lennon. I had grown up on the Beatles and like most of the other kids in my age group was captured within the four young Englishmen's meteoric rise to worldwide super stardom. News of Lennon's tragic death was world news and hit especially hard in his chosen home,

Anthony Belcher

literally gunned down outside his front doorstep. Although it had been a decade or more it felt a lot like the sixties all over again. Here was another man who sang and spoke of peace and love for all mankind violently murdered. Only in America!

There were hundreds of people holding vigils singing "Give Peace A Chance" for weeks after his death. I found myself right in the middle of one of these vigils the night I auditioned for the Artistic Director of the AADA. After the audition I, who hated riding the bus, decided I was going get off after a few blocks and try to find the subway. I ended up walking through Central Park, exiting the park at 72nd Street and Central Park West, which is the location of Lennon's home at the Dakota Apartment building. Lennon had only been dead a couple of days and people were dressed like Hippies and burning candles, many crying, it was beautiful and sad at the same time.

The American Academy of Dramatic Arts is a full-service acting school that covers everything from Mime to Fencing. Originally opening up in 1884 the school has been housed in its current location since 1963 on Park Avenue. The famous Alumni include stars like Danny DeVito (class of 1966), Cleavon Little (class of 1967), as well as those from Hollywood's Golden years

The American

which include the likes of Lauren Bacall (Class of 1942), and Cecil B. DeMille (Class of 1900), just to name a few. I would be attending the night classes every Wednesday from six to ten after work. I enjoyed the classes, even the enunciation exercises consisting of the A E I O OHHHs, and my favorite "The seething sea ceaseth, thus ceasing sufficeth Us", these exercises were part of our weekly warm up and I had fun with them. After class, a bunch of us would meet up at an Irish Bar down the street where we would talk about school and all of the things young actors talk about. Usually by the third pitcher of beer we would be pouring quarters into the Juke Box so we could play and sing along with Frank Sinatra as he crooned about "If I can make It here, I can make it anywhere". The night would end with us in a drunken stumbling chorus line singing the finale "New York New York". There was many a Thursday morning I would show up to work a little hung over.

  I soon fell into the routine of going to work and school. I found New York City, and New Yorkers to be fascinating. I made may daily traverse through the city with wide eyed wonder at its sites and people. I would see my first homeless person, I'm talking about the dressed in tattered clothing, hadn't bathed in months homeless person, who when they entered a train car

Anthony Belcher

everyone else left to go to another car to get away from the funk. I saw for the first time a person with dread locks. These are not the neat stylish locks we see today. This was matted hair that hadn't been combed or washed in years. Where my small-town Midwest sensibilities were shocked by these sights, I was just as disturbed by the nonchalant acceptance they were given by New Yorkers.

In the evenings I would walk around Harlem and revel in the fact that I was living in the most famous black neighborhood in the world. These were the same streets Malcolm preached from. Where Sidney Portier, Harry Belafonte, Duke Ellington, Langston Hughes, Billie Holiday, Sarah Vaughn and many, many others had walked before me. Sadly, I was living in Harlem in 1980-1981. Gone were the glory days when Harlem produced and showcased some of the greatest artist, entertainers, authors, poets, and musicians the world has ever known. In 1980-1981, when I lived in Harlem it was known as the most famous ghetto in the world. I stood in front of the Apollo Theater and cried at its boarded-up windows, and dull rusted marquee. There was a seedy looking liquor store on one side and a cheap strip club on the other. A vision of the album "James Brown Live at The Apollo" flashed through my mind as I remember it being prominently displayed amongst my

The American

grandmother's record collection back on Cedar Street. To stand before this iconic representation of Black American excellence, now in such a sad state broke my heart.

There were some very nice moments I experienced while living in Harlem with the most significant for me being able to read the Auto Biography of Malcolm X by Alex Haley while sitting next to a bust of Malcolm in a little park on Adam Clayton Powell Blvd, (still called Seventh Avenue by native Harlemites) named after Malcolm. My Pops who had been in New York in the early sixties had talked about seeing Malcolm speaking and how powerful he was. I have since read Malcolm's story a number of times, but for a first reading I couldn't have dreamed of a better setting.

At work I was introduced to the world of "Bearer Bonds" As defined by Wikipedia ("A bearer bond is a bond or debt security issued by a business entity such as a corporation or a government. As a bearer instrument, it differs from the more common types of investment securities in that it is unregistered—no records are kept of the owner, or the transactions involving ownership. Whoever physically holds the paper on which the bond is issued is the presumptive owner of the instrument. This is useful for investors who wish to retain anonymity.") I worked

Anthony Belcher

for Paine Webber Jackson & Curtis, (some of you old heads might remember the commercial from the eighties where the tag line was "Thank you Paine Webber"). My first job was to photograph the physical bonds so that they could be transferred to microfilm. I found the job to be interesting as I learned about how cities, states, big companies, and the like all raised and repaid money. I met people of all races and ethnicities, and while they were all different, they were all distinctively New Yorkers. Living in New York I soon began to realize just how culturally ignorant my Midwestern upbringing had left me.

I was shocked and totally ignorant when the first time I was introduced to "Ash Wednesday". I arrived at work that morning where I saw people walking around with what I thought at the time was dirt smeared on their foreheads. I was even more astonished that many of these people were Black!

My ignorance was exposed even further when I realized that almost all of the people from South America were Catholics. I actually called home to ask my mother what was going on. Then there was the time I asked a coworker who happened to be and older Jewish lady that everyone called "Moms" what was the difference between a Puerto Rican and a Mexican. She looked at

The American

me and responded in stereotypical Jewish fashion" Eh, ones from Mexico the other is from Puerto Rico?" and I of course felt like a complete idiot. Then there was the time when an older white gentleman who missed the days when, in his words, "Harlem was safe for White people", asked me if I was sensitive about being black. I responded, "No I had been black all my life".

I realize that today these situations most likely would end up on social media, and there would be many folks up in arms about our ignorance and insensitivity. Back then I think people understood that these types of exchanges between coworkers was how people learned about people. While today my question about Mexicans and Puerto Ricans, along with the question I was asked about being sensitive about being black could very well end up on social media as evidence of mine or his racism and ignorance, back then you had these conversations and that was how you learned to get along with people. In many ways I thought that New York with all of its ethnic neighborhoods, may be the most segregated city in America. Oddly enough I didn't see it as a racist city. Funny thing about people in New York that I noticed while there, was that everybody looks and walks the same during the winter months. The "Hawk" is the great equalizer.

Anthony Belcher

Most nights after work I met with Ms. Jeanette's theater company the H.A.D.L.Y. Players. We were working on a piece that she had written herself or was from a new playwright from the neighborhood. We rehearsed in a theater that was located on Adam Clayton Powell BLVD. that was often without heat. One night while we were rehearsing the actress Butterfly McQueen stopped by. She was far from the scatterbrained subservient characters she had become famous for in movies like "Gone with The Wind". A tiny petite woman, she walked up to the stage wearing a full-length Mink coat and sparkling diamond earrings. A picture of elegance and grace, however the squeaky voice was real. She said in that voice "Ain't you babies cold" and I almost bit my lip off to keep from laughing. The theater was so cold it was actually warmer outside, still we trooped on. Ms. Jeanette got a job with a show being produced by actor Paul Winfield and had to go on the road to St. Louis. I was at her place when he came by to offer her the role and got to meet him. There was a nice moment where after during which we spent some time discussing his interpretation of Walter Lee, as he had assumed the role during a national tour of the play. He autographed my copy of the playbill from the Ft. Wayne production. He seemed to be a regular guy and I enjoyed meeting him.

The American

We stopped working on the piece until Ms. Jeanette returned a few months later, then got back together that spring. One weekend we agreed to meet at one of the cast members place out in Coney Island. The plan was to have a barbecue on the beach do a read through and then go for a swim. It was a beautiful day, and the food was delicious. The reading went well and when we all walked down the beach to the edge of the Atlantic Ocean, I politely refused to do more than get my feet wet. I had seen Jaws!

My first semester would culminate with scene performances for the faculty and student bodies, along with different casting directors and the like from around town. I chose a scene from Does a "Tiger Wear a Necktie?", a play written in 1969 by Don Petersen, and made it's Broadway debut the same year at the Belasco Theater helping to launch the career of actor Al Pacino who was cast as the lead. Mr. Pacino won a Tony award for his performance, and though I of course did not achieve such heights for my performance, I did however get the attention of one of the in-house directors. My scene went well, and it wasn't long after that I was offered a featured role in one of the schools full-fledged productions in the upcoming year. The role was that of a poor boy in a Mexican village who played and sang the guitar. I have looked back at this period of my life over the past twenty

Anthony Belcher

years of being of "sober mind" with wonder, anger, frustration, and finally a profound sadness at what might have been. The offer scared me to death! It was known to all and especially to me that I could not play guitar, not to mention that I was terrified of having to sing in front of people. I had lost the blind courage and confidence I had when I bumbled though "Take me out to the ball game" back at Ft. Wayne Civic. I turned the role down flat.

We went right into our next quarter without break. My classmates and I were all excited about the next steps having had our first taste of performing. We would have a different instructor for this term as the instructor that guided us through first phase had either gone off to LA or gotten work on one of the productions in New York. Almost from the beginning of classes the new instructor didn't seem to care for me much and was always very critical of my scene work. I couldn't seem to do anything right in her eyes. One day after an exercise that I was probably late too, she decided to dress me down in front of the class. Going on to say how she thought that I thought I was better than my classmates and too smart to learn anything from her. It was a very personal attack. Her comments were cruel and meanspirited. They also echoed those old negative feelings that I had always carried around in my bag of life. I didn't think I was

THE AMERICAN

better than my classmates, though I did fell that I was beginning to stand out in the class. Her words only confirmed all of the negative feelings I had about myself. Feelings that said that I was a fraud, that I was not worthy. If it wasn't that day, it was shortly after that I quit school.

Throughout my time in New York, I had been sending out pictures and resumes through Backstage Magazine as defined by Wikipedia (is an entertainment-industry brand aimed at people working in film and the performing arts, with a special focus on casting, job opportunities, and career advice.) During my time Backstage was the primary way professional actors found work. I had friend who took my first set of headshots, and I found a photo shop nearby that gave a good price on reprints and I sent out an average of five or ten sets a week to companies all over the country. They of course had all of the listings for stage and tv performances in New York, but also plenty of road shows that were produced throughout the country listed their openings as well.

One Saturday morning there was a knock on my door, by my neighbor telling me that I had a phone call. Still half asleep I stumbled down to the phone to take the call. On the phone

Anthony Belcher

was a man named Bill. He was from Phoenix Arizona, and he owned a national touring company. He was casting for his latest production of "Treasure Island" that would tour Illinois, Indiana, Kentucky, and Tennessee. The shows would perform in High Schools throughout those states, and he was offering me the part of "Jimmy Hawkins". If I accepted, he would fly me to Phoenix for the rehearsals after which we would drive back to Chicago for our first show. The job paid $150. 00 per week plus lodgings and meals. I was not really excited about the offer, which Bill seemed to notice and commented on. I explained it away by saying that I had just woke up and was still absorbing the idea that I had been offered a job. I asked him how much time I had before I needed to be in Phoenix, and he told me a week. I told him I could be ready by then and he said that he would get back to me with the flight information. After finishing up the call I went back to my room and sat on my bed to think about what had just happened. My initial feeling was that this was not the great opportunity that Mr. Bill from Phoenix was making it out to be. Still, I thought, with all that had happened at school, and the fact that we were running into financial issues with getting Ms. Jeanette's show up and running. Add to all of that the fact I had gotten involved with a married woman at work, whose husband had actually busted

The American

in on us recently while I was spending the night with her at her mother's house. We fought pretty much to a draw that night, but that seemed not to satisfy him. He was now stalking me. He had showed up at work looking form me recently, and a couple of days prior to the phone call I was told he had been to the Y looking for me. Considering everything it seemed to me that getting out of New York right now wasn't such a bad idea.

After talking to Ms. Jeanette who acknowledge that it probably wasn't a top production, but it was a chance to get paid as an actor, as well as a valuable opportunity to learn more about my craft. I gave them a week notice at my job, sold my little black and white TV which other than my clothes were all the possessions I had. Exactly one week after receiving Bill's call I boarded a United Airlines flight at JFK and was headed to Phoenix Arizona.

Bill met me at the airport. My first impression of Phoenix was the heat. It was early September, and it was still ninety degrees outside at six o'clock in the evening. He explained the set up to me as we drove to the motel. He told me my partner had arrived earlier in the week and I would meet him on Monday. Partner? I asked what he meant by that and that is when he

Anthony Belcher

explained to me that his company booked two-man shows in elementary schools throughout the country. We would not only perform "Treasure Island", but we would also do "The Prince and the Pauper. We would only be portraying a couple of the characters which each of us taking on dual roles. There would be no director, stagehands, or crew of any sort. All of our sets were portable pop-ups and along with our costumes would fit into a small covered pickup truck. We would drive from city to city to make our performance dates and would share the driving responsibilities.

When I finally got settled into the motel room that night, I went to sleep thinking I had just left New York, where regardless of the negative experience I had at school, and the cold theater we had to use for rehearsals, even the angry husband who was looking to bash my head in, was a far better situation than I found myself in now. I had joined a Puppet Show using live people and I was one of the Puppets!

We finished up the rehearsals after about three weeks and in early October then set out for Chicago and our first show. I had met Frank, my partner who was an upper middle class white kid from Westchester New York. He too, wasn't really happy

The American

with the situation, but we were young actors, and we figured this experience was part of paying our proverbial dues. During the drive from Phoenix, we didn't talk much, he seemed to be a bit aloof, towards me, and we mostly talked about movies and music during the two days it took us to get there.

We arrived in Chicago and had our first performance. To my surprise the show went really well, and the kids absolutely enjoyed it. After the show Frank informed me that he would be quitting the show and heading back to New York. I asked if he called Bill and he said he did not and asked if I would after dropping him off at O'Hare. I did, and Bill cussed and fussed about the news then told me he would have another guy out in a couple of days.

My next partner was a guy named Ben who was also an upper middle classed kid from Westchester. As was the case with both of these guys I had not spent this much time with a white person of any class before in my life. I am pretty sure that neither Ben nor Frank had been in a situation where they were stuck in a truck with a black kid from the projects in Indiana either. I only write this now because in today's world so much is made about "cultural" differences. As with my first partner, Frank, Ben

Anthony Belcher

and I talked about the movies, and music. There were no real adjustments for either of us to get along with the other due to the differences in our races. Ben was really knowledgeable about the history of the American theater and knew all of the hit tunes from all of the big Broadway productions. There were differences between us, but they were not cultural. We were both products of the American culture. Our differences? I was into sports, and he was not. He was gay and I was not. He grew up with money and I grew up broke as a bag of glass.

Culturally, we were both born in the fifties and part of the American culture of the sixties and seventies. None of this is to say that the three months we spent together in that truck and sharing hotel rooms did not present some situations that we had to address. One such incident occurred while I was watching a Bears game on TV. We were still in Chicago and were lucky enough to have found a suite that fit our budget.

The suite was set up where the bedroom with the two beds was separate from the common area. Ben walked out of the shower and for whatever reason decided that he needed to get something from the common area and pranced butt naked right in front of the TV. Later, maybe even years later I thought

THE AMERICAN

that he may have been making a pass at me. At the time though, my only response was "Hey Man Get Your Naked Ass Out of Here". He seemed to just realize that he was naked and scurried back to the bed area. There was no big fight or any period of uncomfortableness on my part and I didn't detect any on his.

There was another occasion later during the tour when we were in Memphis Tennessee. I had met a young lady and brought her back to the room after a night at the local Juke Joint. We didn't have the luxury of a room with a common area and instead had a regular motel room with double beds. It was after midnight, and I figured Ben would be fast asleep and would never know we were there. The young lady and I had gotten into some heavy petting when the light comes on and Ben is laying there with his head propped in his hand going really? Of course, the young lady as well as I felt embarrassed and we both apologized, and I took her home.

Neither of these incidents caused any lasting tension between us and we never brought them up again once we had addressed them. The only incidents that occurred that highlighted our different races had little to do with us and more to do with where we were at the time. After another show in Chicago, we got

Anthony Belcher

stuck behind an accident on Michigan Ave on the South Side of Chicago. It was a warm early October day and what had happened ahead of us had brought traffic to a complete stop. There were people out on the streets talking loudly, blowing their horns, and expressing their frustration with the traffic. It was unseasonably warm, and we had the windows down. A bee flew into the cab of the truck and Ben lost it. He started screaming and swatting at the bee and jumped straight out of the car onto Michigan Ave. He was only out there for a second as he noticed that all of the Black people where now staring directly at him. He said "Oh Shit" sort of quietly and jumped back into the truck and killed the bee. This tickled me to the point of incapacitation. I was laughing so hard tears were streaming down my face.

I could hear people shouting and complaining all around me as the traffic had started to move however, I was caught up in a laughing fit and couldn't move. It didn't help matters that Ben who had quieted down after killing the bee was now screaming at me to move the damn car before I got him killed, which only caused me to laugh even harder.

We were booked into a school in Gary Indiana. As was our pattern we arrived at the school and went to the office to find out

The American

where to set up. As we were walking through the hallways, I began to notice that the students seemed to be in class or something because I didn't see any children in the hallways. In fact, most of the people I saw in the hallways all seemed pretty close to my age. When we entered the office, I asked the secretary what the average age of their students was. She looked at me a little strangely before replying "Honey most of the kids are older than you" She went on to explain that this was an adult school for people who for various reasons were kicked out of the public school system, or were pregnant, or had been pregnant. I asked could I use her phone and called Bill explaining what we were faced with. I told him that I had concerns about trying to perform "Treasure Island" for a group of high school dropouts in Gary Indiana. Bill feigned not knowing that this was not an elementary and school and basically said that they paid for a show, and we would have to give them a show. I hung up the phone and turned to Ben who had been standing beside me hoping there was some sort of mistake. He looked at me with that question mark look people have and said okay what's happening? I said basically we are gonna get killed.

By this time, the principle had gotten involved and assured us both that with his addressing the students before we went

Anthony Belcher

on, he could smooth it over for us. I was totally against this idea, mostly because right away I felt that the principle was pompous asshole who only cared about himself and his programs. I instinctively knew that if he went up before us, he'd suck out all of the energy and leave me to perform before a pissed off audience. The space we were to use was really small, with the front row of the audience right up against the lip of the raised platform that was acting as a stage. The crowd was assembled and there were some pretty hard looking characters amongst them that wasn't lost on Ben. Due to the shortage of space we had to stand just behind him to his left where we could be seen by the students but not by, he and his staff. Just as I suspected he was sucking all of the positive energy out of the room, and we could see the students begin to get angry. I began to mock him behind his back which the students got a big kick out of. Even more so when he thought that their laughing and clapping was meant for him. We finally got him off stage. I went up and explained what we were doing and how much we appreciated them allowing us to perform for them. The antics with the principle had worked and we had them from the opening scene.

Right up until the time in the piece where Ben is supposed to roll a black cane out from backstage to signify the impending

The American

arrival of the pirate Long John Silver. Maybe it was nerves, but whatever the reason Ben tossed the cane instead of rolling it and it bounced and hit a very mean looking brother in the leg that was sitting in the front row. He jumped to his feet, and I immediately broke character and said, "naw man naw man he didn't mean it" The other students who had gotten into the show joined in yelling it was an accident man, sit down so we can finish the show. The angry brother looked around then chuckled and sat back down I went right back into character. We finished the show and got a nice round of applause.

The rest of the tour was pretty much uneventful we missed a couple of shows due to my poor management or Bill's tough schedule. There were many days we would finish a late afternoon show and would have a four maybe five-hour drive to our next city. This usually meant that we had already performed a morning show and by the end of the second we would be exhausted, and I would elect to get something to eat, get a room so we could rest and get an early start in the morning. Most of the time this would work out and a couple of times it didn't. We spent the last of the tour in Tennessee, and Kentucky finishing up in Lexington. Ben decided that he would fly back to New York from Lexington and I who had planned to go onto LA, would drive the truck back

Anthony Belcher

to Phoenix. It took me about two and a half days to drive back to Phoenix and after spending the night and settling up with Bill I caught a Greyhound bus to Los Angeles. I arrived in LA in January of 1982. It was a beautiful Southern California evening. Dad picked me up at the bus station and we drove to Aunt Gladys's house. I had already spoken to my cousin Elgin who had his own place in Long Beach, and he agreed to let me sleep on his couch.

During my long drive and subsequent bus ride I had plenty of time to think about turning down the featured role I had been offered at AADA and knew I could have played the role and played it well. New York was behind me as were all of the bad mistakes I had made. I had regained some confidence in my talent and felt better about my future as an actor. I would hit the ground running and started doing extra work almost right away. I hooked up with a young actor named Del Zamora after we were both cast in a student film. He kept me up to date on what was going on and when he was cast in the Emilio Esteves move "Repo Man", he got me an audition. I would come to learn that cold readings and improvisation was not my strong points. My audition was terrible; however, I still got a couple of days work as background. I also got to hang out in the trailer with Del and met the now late actress Vonetta McGee, who had been a big star in the seventies

THE AMERICAN

black-exploitation movies and had a co-starring role. Del, was very confident in his talent and more importantly was willing to do whatever it took to be successful. He lived in his Van with his little white dog. His only focus was on acting. He was determined not to have to take a "day" job and lived on his acting work. I know now that he loved the craft. Del possessed the one thing that I did not. Belief that he deserved the best life he could give himself. He deserved to have a career in whatever field he chose. Because of his belief in his ability, and his dedication to his craft, Del would go on to have roles in big hits like "Robo Cop" "Born in East LA" and to my pleasant surprise a reoccurring role for a season in HBO's "True Blood". Because of my lack of these characteristics, it would be twenty years before I would be able to think in the same way.

I started smoking weed every day the day I arrived at Norton Air Force Base way back in October of 1974. I wasn't on base for more than an hour before I brought my first ounce. From that point on I smoked weed every day and would continue to do so until the first time I would go into treatment in 1987. I also had tried every new, or fad drug that had come out during that time. Drugs more or less became my primary source of recreation. I didn't really hang out with anyone who didn't get high. I tried

Anthony Belcher

everything that came out. I snorted Heroin and Cocaine, I smoked Angel Dust, I dropped pills I took Acid. The people I hung out with all did drugs. They were all working class people, but there were a group of us that seeking out and doing drugs was how we spent our time when we weren't working. Of all of these people I was the most committed to this lifestyle. Ironically enough, if you told me back then that I was an Addict, I would have laughed in your face and told you that the difference between us, and "real drug addicts" we were people who controlled our drug use, while the "real addicts" allowed the drugs to control them. That is what I might have said to you then. Today I would say that back then all of my responses regarding drugs was pretty much typical dope fiend bullshit! Drugs were about to take over my life and help me to finally prove to myself that I was what I thought I was a bad person who wasn't worthy of a successful life.

I spent my last few months in LA going thorough what I now have deemed to be one of my depression stages. I wasn't getting much work, my relationship wasn't working out, I had lost my job. Life kinda just sucked. I got a call to audition for a part in a play that was being produced in one of the small West Hollywood theaters. I don't remember anything about the play, its name or the people involved, but what I do remember is that I finally gave

The American

a decent audition. It came down to me and one other guy for the role. The director wanted me, and the producer wanted the other guy. The producer won. I was pretty much devastated by not getting the role, and disillusion began to set in, and I started to question if moving to LA had been the right decision for me. After a big fight with my girlfriend, I decided it was time to put LA behind me and head back to New York. The plan was that I would make a short stop in Ft. Wayne for a few months so that I could get a job, save some money, see the kids and family before moving on to New York.

Finding a job wasn't turning out to be as easy as I thought. Ft. Wayne, like many Midwestern cities of its size had been hit hard by Reganomics and the decline of blue-collar jobs. Most of the work I got was of the telemarketing kind. Telemarking is something I had picked up while living in LA. The schedules were pretty flexible, and the only skill set needed was the ability to talk to people. Also, like restaurants it was one of the few places where you could get hired and start the next day. Telemarketing replaced restaurants as my go to job, meaning if push came to shove, I could always find work as a telemarketer.

I would finally catch on with a home repair company

Anthony Belcher

whose primary product was Solar Panels. Back then the federal government offered a very nice tax refund to those who renovated their homes using solar energy as a power source. The Ft. Wayne office of the company had a five-man sales team which was supported by a smoked filled, coffee-stained room full of about twenty people. This set up is known, or at least was known back then as a "Boiler Room". My job was to make cold calls to set up appointments for the salespeople to visit the customer's home and demonstrate or "pitch" our products. I was promoted to Manager a few months after starting the job and for a short time things went really well. After the tax credit ended, layoffs followed, and the company had to shut down the "Boiler Room". They switched products and we began to sell the newest technological advance in home entertainment, known back then as "Satellite TV"! I took a chance a took the offer to go into direct sales.

    I was a better salesman than I was a boiler room manager, and it wasn't long before I was making good money. I had met and become serious with a woman who would become my second wife. My dream of being an actor was slowly being pushed to the rear of my priority list. I began to look at my life differently. I had a good paying job with room for advancement where I wore a shirt and tie to work. I was in love with a woman who was both

THE AMERICAN

beautiful and respected within the community. I started to lie to myself about my acting aspirations, telling myself that I would get back to it in a couple of years.

Queen Esther and I were married and for the next couple of years my life became what I had aways wanted it to be. I had a good job and a good woman. We had seven kids between us with her girls being the oldest at 15 and 16. I was even able to get back into the local theatre scene landing roles in productions at the Indiana/Purdue University campus.

The most successful and most challenging for me was "Ain't Misbehavin", the Broadway musical that celebrates the music of Jazz/Swing music great Fats Waller. I had a solo performance singing the "Vipers Drag" a song that celebrates the weed smokers of Wallers day. Talk about type casting. Despite my nightly anxiety about having to sing, we had a really good cast, and the show was a big hit. The other piece we did was "Ceremonies of Dark Old Men" a two-act play written by Lonnie Elder III and first produced by the Negro Ensemble Company. This production was special as my baby brother William was cast to play my brother in the show. Fred Jackson, a good friend of my Pops who also was known around Ft. Wayne as a jazz drummer

Anthony Belcher

was cast in the role as the father. I had spent many years sitting in Pop's apartment soaking up wisdom from him and Fred. I had recommended Fred for the role, and he auditioned and was cast. Our opening night was a disaster and I being the "star" took most of the blame for the bad performance. We got it together for the next night and enjoyed a successful run after that.   At work, I had found that Satellite TV technology was an easy item for me to sell. The cost of cable tv was getting more and more expensive and the idea that you could get everything that cable TV offered with your own device was appealing to many. I not only flourished but would become the company's top salesman. Sales is where I seemed to find my niche. Most of my customers were White and lived in the small towns surrounding Ft. Wayne. I made thirty thousand in sales my first moth. My clientele were White and rural. With the exception of a couple of occasions I can honestly say that the fact that I was black had no affect one way or the other on my success. A good salesperson, especially those doing direct sales in the home, have to have the ability to make a connection with their perspective client. Many do so by engaging the client in stories. I was good at telling stories. I made sure that my stories connected with the morals and values of my perspective customers.

THE AMERICAN

America was a different place back then. We were the generation that John Kennedy had challenged Americans to "ask not what our country could do for us but ask what we could do for our country". The proverbial silver lining that lies within the bloody, turbulent, dark cloud that was the sixties was that Americans, in particularly Americans of different races made an honest attempt to get along. In doing so we collectively made the country better. Not only for Black folks, but for Women, the Gay and Lesbian community, as well as people with disabilities, all who's respective movements were based in the overall Civil rights movement as it metamorphosed into a world-wide Human rights movement.   Most importantly Black folk were not viewed as negatively as they are today especially Black men. A case in point is the story of Mohammad Ali, who during the sixties and early seventies had been one of the most hated of Black men by White Americans. After the fiasco of that was the Vietnam war, and the unfairness in the position the government took against him. Ali was now seen as a courageous and heroic figure. Of course, there are those who would argue that the change in White Americas attitudes toward Ali was only because he had been retired from the ring for over a decade and had long ago stopped talking shit and knocking out White boys. Also, by the time the ninety-six

Anthony Belcher

summer Olympics came around which featured Ali lighting the ceremonial torch, he was showing the beginning of Parkinson's disease and had all but lost his ability to speak.

I am by no means saying that the old prejudices and attitudes whites have historically held regarding Black folk in general and particularly Black men didn't still exist. However, I am saying that these attitudes were not openly promoted and accepted. I believe the chipping away at the positive views of Black men that came as a result of the movements of the sixties and early seventies began with Ronald Reagan's campaign add about "Welfare Queens". Mr. Regan with his "ask yourself if you are better off today than you were four years ago" challenge, followed by Gordon Gecko, a character played by Michael Douglas in the movie "Wall Street", telling Americans that "Greed is Good" ushering the "Me" generation that followed.

Regan's campaign adds which not so subtlety painted the picture that Black Americans were committing massive welfare fraud, while White Americans paid for this through higher taxes. Gordon Gecko's mantra helped to fray the fabric of morality standards in not only business but also the collective American psyche. Then along came the "Crack" epidemic, the rise

The American

and promotion of "Gang" culture and "Gangsta Rap" all shown in glorious living color on the evening news promoting to the world that Black men are dangerous. White America as much as they loved Michael Jordan, Michael Jackson, Eddie Murphy, and other Black superstars, was afraid of Black men, because Black men were dangerous! The next generation of Americans would see the American prison population grow to be largest in the world. A prison system whose population in which more than half of its inmates would be Black Americans. Unfortunately, I would be one of them.

When I walked out of the house, I was surprised at how late it was. It was a brisk October night, and I pulled my coat up around the collar as I walked to my car parked down the street. I turned back to look at the house thinking that might change something, but there it was, the old gnarled three with its branches hanging over the doorway. The place looked like a house from one of the latest slasher movies. I looked at my watch and thought damn! I ain't got no money and it's too late to get some. I checked my pockets being sure to carefully go through the inside pockets on the new leather coat I was wearing. Then I looked at the watch again, which was also new. For a moment I stood in the street not sure of what I was going to do next. Finally, I shook my head

Anthony Belcher

and said "no" to myself and made my way to the car. I got in the car and pulled off, not really knowing where I was going or what I was going to do next. I rubbed the lapel on my coat and looked at my watch again then chuckled a little. I looked up and realized that I had been driving in a circle and was approaching the corner where the house was located. I parked the car and went back inside. When I left the house again the sun had come up and I was without my leather coat and new watch. As I got in the car, I caught a glimpse of my face in the rearview mirror and said out loud for the first time. "Man, you a dope fiend"

After making salesman of the month, I partnered up with a guy named Steve. Steve was known as a closer and though I had just come off a great month on my own, I thought that teaming up with him would make us both stronger. Our sales manager was against the paring because he felt that I didn't need a partner. I knew Steve from our telemarking days, and he lived not too far from me, so the partnership worked on many levels. The primary one being our love of cocaine. From about May through August of nineteen eighty-six, we set records for units sold, as well as total revenues brought into the company. We averaged close to three confirmed sales per week. The average unit cost was between three and five thousand dollars of which our commission was

The American

ten percent. By the time August of that year rolled around our production had taken a deep downturn and both of us were having problems at home due to our addition. We had also began getting our drugs fronted and had taken some drugs on credit from a couple of dealers.

According to Steve, there was this Detroit connected dealer who had fronted us an eighth of an ounce, which was about three hundred dollars, and was demanding payment that day and if we didn't pay him someone was going to be hurt. Knowing neither of us had the money Steve showed up at my place that morning insisting that we needed to go into hiding. He suggested we enroll ourselves in a twenty-one-day treatment center. I wasn't really concerned as I knew we could make the money in one sale, and there was also the fact that these were Steve's connections and thus his problem. Such is the loyalty of drug addicts. The truth for me was that I was just tired. There was a part of me that knew that the success I was experiencing and the life I was building with Queen Ester and the kids was the life that I had long wanted and was the proof that the voice inside my head was wrong about me not being worthy. The other part of me knew that all of my success at home and at work was a façade and the real me, the me behind the voice was determined to destroy me.

Anthony Belcher

Steve and I entered the drug program in one of the local hospitals. The guy in charge of the program, was a counselor named Matt who after finishing our intake paperwork stated" alright you two dope fiends follow me" as he led us to our rooms. We both stiffened at his comments but kept walking. I called my wife and told her that I was trying to do something about my drug problem and let her know that she couldn't visit for about a week because of the mandatory "blackout" which amounted to no contact from anyone outside of the program the first week. This was a standard in all programs of its time. These were the days of hospital programs, so the accommodations were hospital clean and organized. The staff were nurses and aids who were very polite and professional. We were treated like patients. It really was a nice place. The next day after breakfast Steve checked out. I decided to stay.

I was introduced to the world of 12 step programs. Back then AA (Alcoholics Anonymous), was the established and most prominent group. However, drug addiction in the states had been on the rise since the Vietnam war, sparking the birth of NA (Narcotics Anonymous), which was just beginning to grow nationwide. I went to the meetings, listened, and participated in the groups. Though I basically agreed with all that I heard in

The American

these meetings, I would not even consider the concept of total abstinence from all mind-altering substances. I believed that I had a problem with cocaine, but totally rejected the idea that I could not go back to smoking weed daily and drinking beer on occasion There are three incidents from my first attempt at getting clean that sick out in my memories.

On my counselor's suggestion, mom agreed to come in so that I could confront her about how I felt about everything. It was a total disaster. I spent an hour screaming incoherently at my mother about everything from the circumstances of my birth, her selection of boyfriends, to her parenting choices in general. It was not a conversation as much as it was a venting session for me. I never considered Moms side of the story. What I know now about how understanding why she made the choices she did, could help me understand that her decisions were not made because of me, but more so they were made because of the circumstances of her life.

Mom was brought up in a generation that believed that the decisions parents made for their children was not their children's business and they shouldn't dare to question those decisions. She didn't actually say that it wasn't my business, but instead said if it were up to her, I would never have found out the truth. That she totally ignored the fact that I only found out the truth because she got drunk and spilled the beans herself served to infuriate me further.

As I look back at this time now, I realize that because neither one of us knew how to have a healthy conversation about my issues this first attempt only pushed us further apart instead of bringing us closer together. The other incident was that I got a chance to talk to Dad. The conversation went differently and to this day I can't say for sure the reason it went differently was because the little boy inside me was still terrified of Dad. While I can say now that being afraid of Dad may have played a role in my approach to the conversation, I am certain today that I was not as angry at Dad as I was at Mom. For in my mind, it wasn't Dad who had betrayed me, it was Mom who had betrayed me, and I was sure she had betrayed him as well.

I was meeting with Dad because I felt I needed make amends to him because of the hatred that I thought I felt toward him growing up. Our conversation took place during the ride back to the facility after a weekend pass. When I finished my spiel, he said, that I didn't owe him, and apology and he didn't really

The American

remember what he did during his drinking days. It was like he had punched me in the gut and for a moment I believe I was actually gasping for air. Did he just say he didn't remember all of the ugly shit he had did to me and my brothers and sisters?

The little boy in me screamed in anger inside my head "You don't remember? What do you mean you don't remember, I thought. I Remember Every Fucking Minute of It!" I felt it was so unfair. I had been erased. The real me stood there in shock and allowed the conversation to drift off to something else. The other incident that has stuck with me since that time was that one of the nurses told me that most of the staff thought that I was superficial and could not be really sincere about anything or anyone. This hurt me so very deeply. It too was a gut shot, only it was accompanied by a kick in the nuts. What hurt the most is that it was exactly what I felt about me too.

My first week back to work I sold two units. I brought an ounce of weed to celebrate. I hadn't gotten high all week. I went to the basement and lit the joint. About halfway through I started to get really depressed. I began to think what I had been told about complete abstinence from all mind-altering substances, while I was in the program. I thought that it was just a matter

Anthony Belcher

of time before I would be back to smoking crack. I could hear the nurse saying they all think you are superficial. That the nice charming funny guy you present to everyone is only a cover for something very dark inside. For the first time in my life, I thought that I should just kill myself.

I had been experiencing Suicidal Ideation for a number of years prior to that day. I had long believed that I would not live past thirty and 1986 was the year in which I would turn thirty. A month after leaving treatment I relapsed and re-entered the same program I had just left. I would stay only two weeks. After leaving the program, I took a position with a different company and once again did well. About my third week with this company, I set a record for sales made. To celebrate I went on a weekend long binge that once I had come down left me deeply depressed. I sat there thinking that this was a good day as any to end it. It wasn't a planned attempt and I looked around the basement for something to do the deed. I found a can of liquid Drano and fixed myself a cocktail of Drano and Water and drank about half of it down. After a few seconds I thought "Okay, this is a really stupid idea" and went upstairs to tell my wife I needed to be taken to the emergency room.

The American

By the time we arrived at the hospital I was spitting up a little blood. When the hospital staff began to ask me what happened my responses sounded like they were coming from Donald Duck. They put something down my throat, and I threw up more blood and blacked out. When I woke up, I was in a hospital room with a tube stuck down my nose. I found myself on the psychiatric ward for the first time. After about a week they decided that I wasn't crazy, I was just a little fucked up and they let me out. The next day, I entered into a long-term program.

Ninety-day programs back then were considered long term treatment. The program was located in Richmond Indiana home to the state mental health facility. I stayed clean a few weeks after that before relapsing and running away to Mansfield Ohio where I stayed with my grandfather and Greg for about a month before going back home. Shortly after that I left again telling Esther that I needed to try to start my life over somewhere other than Ft. Wayne and moved to Norristown Pennsylvania to stay with my brother Amos and his family. I got a job in a country club and things went well for maybe two months. My Great Aunt Elsie passed away and Amos and I made the drive from Norristown to Mansfield to attend her funeral.

Anthony Belcher

It was good to see Moms side of the family. From Uncle Bobby to Uncle Jimmy, they all were great story tellers and big laughers. Mom's cousin Bishop Jerome Ross of Columbus Ohio presided over the funeral. One day Greg and I stopped in the bank and as we passed a few guys on our way in he said to me "there goes your brother", I looked up expecting to ask Bug what he was doing there and instead came face to face with a short man of about thirty-five. I looked at Greg and he said its Dennis. I hadn't seen Dennis in about fifteen years when Granny had brought him to the house one Thanksgiving. He knew who Greg was and spoke to him. He looked at me for a few minutes he said, "You are one of my brothers" and walked up to me and gave me a hug. I broke out in tears. I remember crying all the way back to where the family had gathered at Aunt Elsie's and telling Mom that we needed to do something about bringing Dennis back into the family. She responded that we would, but I didn't really believe her. After the funeral services Amos and I drove back to Norristown. I didn't know it then, but it would be almost twenty years before I would see Denis again.

After the movie I asked my date if she knew where we could get some coke. She did, and we did. The night ended with me parked in a field before an old decrepit barn finishing off a

The American

bottle of Hennessey, I had taken from bugs liquor cabinet. After taking the last swig from the bottle I threw it out the window then reached into the glove compartment and pulled out a box cutter and slit my wrist. It was a deep cut and began to bleed pretty good. I sat there watching the blood slowly turn the sleave of the white shirt I was wearing red.

I began to look at the barn doors and think how it would be great fun to crash the car through the doors like they were doing in all of the action movies that were coming out at the time. I had started to cry. The tears strolling down my face blurring my vision as I looked at the door. I put the car in gear and pressed the gas pedal to the floor. A moment later the wooded doors shattered into splinters as I drove into and through them. I crashed through the door and hit the center beam. I felt the car bounced back a little. I thought that it would be even cooler to crash through the beam and bring the whole roof down. I put the car in reverse backed up a way and then floored it driving head on into the center beam screaming die motha fucka die!

When I came to, I was in the back seat lying partially on the floor. I could hear this popping sound all around me. I sat up and realized that the car was on fire. I looked closer and realized

Anthony Belcher

that the car, the barn, and the grass were all on fire. I walked out of the inferno that had still been a barn when I drove up. I noticed the police car that was parked on the road. The officer who was looking at me as if he was seeing a ghost. My arm was now caked with dried blood. The officer slowly got out of the car. I don't remember if I was handcuffed. All I remember saying is that I didn't start that fire after which I passed out. To this day I cannot offer a logical explanation for why I didn't die in that fire. It was truly a miracle and I believe an act of God.

When I came to, I was handcuffed to a gurney. Someone was pulling my arm. I remember trying to sit up and realizing I was restrained. I began to scream "You motha fucka's need to let me go" I looked around the room and saw my brother Amos. I will never forget the look on his face which was twisted in anguish and horror. I was a raving maniac screaming incoherently at all around me. I blacked out again. The next time I woke up I was in another Psych ward. After a couple of days Esther, whom Bug had sent for came to visit me. I promised I would get my shit together and come back to Ft. Wayne. First, I had to deal with the courts. To my luck the barn and the land it was on was owned by the Nuclear Power plant down the street and was scheduled for demolition anyway. Turns out I had done them a favor, and they

The American

were not inclined to pursue criminal charges.

The Commonwealth of Pennsylvania had other ideas, and I would be sentenced to six months to be served in the Montgomery County Correctional Facility. I would spend close to four months there before being released. After a night with Bug, I caught the bus back to Ft. Wayne and for the next year and half I was drug free and from all appearances had put all of those dark days behind me.

The following year I kept my promise to Queen Esther and came back to Ft. Wayne. Drug and Alcohol free I got a part-time job working at K-Mart and enrolled at IPFW as a theater major. That first-year life was good, and I was happy. The negative voice that constantly haunted me in my head was quiet. I was able to repair a lot of the damage I had done to my reputation and be a real father to my kids and step kids. I played ball with my boys and attended school functions, and parent/teacher conferences. I helped out with homework and put together movie nights. It was a time in my life that I would look back upon during the dark years to remind myself that I was not a total piece of shit.

I completed my first year of school with a B average and prepared to enter my second year. Queen Esther announced that

Anthony Belcher

she was pregnant and in July of 1989 we welcomed her fifth and my fourth child, a wide-eyed baby girl we called Danielle. I continued to do well in school and when I was asked, I agreed to take on a roll in the school production of "Sizwe Bonzi is Dead" (Sizwe Banzi Is Dead is a play by Athol Fugard, written collaboratively with two South African actors, John Kani and Winston Ntshona. Goodreads 3.9/5). I also had changed jobs having left K-Mart to work graveyard shift as a short order cook at one of the local diners. After leaving work I would get home just before Esther had to leave for work and would watch the baby until the sitter came by around ten am to pick her up. I would then try to get in a couple hours sleep before making it to school for my afternoon classes. Between work, rehearsals, and watching Danni, the schedule was brutal leaving me tired and irritable most of the time. I began to question the practicality of what I would do once I graduated with a degree in Theater Arts. I knew I didn't want to teach, and I certainly didn't want to go after a master's degree. The depression deepened and I began to have those old feelings again. I began feeling that everybody was demanding this and that of me, but nobody really cared about me or how I felt.

There is an acronym used in recovery circles called HALT. Never get to Hungry, Angry, Lonely, or Tired. The idea is to remind

The American

addicts to monitor how they are feeling and be able to recognize emotions that make them vulnerable to relapse. The underlying message is to never allow yourself to become "too" anything emotionally. Of course, I didn't know any of this at the time. About three weeks prior to the night, I would literally sit in my car and decide to throw my life away, I had smoked a joint at work. One of the cooks offered to share a joint with me during break. We had just handled our Friday rush of customers who wanted food after the clubs closed. The fact that I wanted to smoke a joint after not getting high at all for over eighteen months, is something that today I would recognize as a sign that something was wrong. That I was "off my spot" a phrase I would pick up in the many prisons I did not yet know would become a part of my coming future. Had I a crystal ball that night allowing me to see that what I was contemplating doing would set me on a path that would see me spend nine of the next twelve years in various prisons, I might have made a different choice.

  I sat outside the restaurant and quickly went over in my mind how I was going to make the manager give me the money in the safe. I decided I would walk in through the lobby into the kitchen. I would pick up a knife from the rack that sat over the sink, then call the manager to the office. Once I had him in the

Anthony Belcher

office, I would show him the knife and make him open the safe and give me the money. I knew that they had just finished with their evening rush and would only have a couple of wait staff on along with a cook and the manager. I walked into the store and responded politely to the waitress who greeted me with a "what's up Tony" I waved at her and kept walking. For a second when I got to the knife rack the only knife hanging there was the one that the tip was broken off. For another second, I considered not going through with my plan, but quickly decided I had come too far to turn back. I grabbed the broken knife and proceeded to the office door. The manager was already there I knocked on the door and he waved me in. Once inside I shut the door and brandished the knife. I said to him "Open the safe man, I won't ask again" and moved closer to him. He said, "quick joking around man this isn't funny". I hit him in the chest with a straight stabbing motion hard enough to make him fall back into his seat. He checked to see if he was bleeding then reached over and pushed the door to the safe open and motioned for me to get what I wanted. I reached in and grabbed the wad of bills that were sitting in plain view and turned and walked outside into the crowded parking lot. I had just robbed my own place of employment.

I knew the police were going to be looking for me and had

The American

left the car parked in the parking lot of the Target store located in the same strip mall as my now former place of employment. I ran into a couple of smokers that were leaving the Target store just as I was exiting the restaurant and jumped in the car with them. We went to one their places and smoked until all the money was gone. It was now about four am and I believe I was walking back to the car. I was pretty much wacked out of my head and when I saw the schoolhouse, I thought it a good idea to break in and rob it. I broke in through a back window quickly found the locked desk which most likely held the cash. I struck out to find something to break the lock with. I ended up walking around the entire school, before coming back to the desk and seeing the big red fire extinguisher hanging on the wall right above the it. It took me only a couple of whacks before the lock gave and I found the couple of hundred bucks they had in cash. I shut the drawer stood up and heard. "THIS IS THE POLICE WE ARE COMING IN!" Shit! I was caught!

    I ran out of the office and up the stairs. I looked out a window and saw that the school was surrounded. I ran out of the classroom I was in and looked down the stairwell. I could see the flashlights beaming off the walls as the police mounted the stairs. I ran into another classroom looking for somewhere

Anthony Belcher

to hide. Finally, I hid in a closet. The German Sheppard Police dog growled in my face as the officer holding him looked at me and said, "okay it's over come on out of there." I came out of the closet and was cuffed and taken downtown to be booked. I was actually going through the booking process in the police garage and hadn't entered the jail outright just yet. The booking officer didn't re-cuff me when I was handed over to him. He was also walking with a very bad limp. The thought ran through my mind that if I ran this dude had no chance of catching me. Though I was all but out on my feet when the garage door opened, I bolted. The chase didn't last long a few blocks at best before I just stopped and gave up. They marched me back into the jail and I passed out.

When I woke up, I was a prisoner of the Allen County Jail. After about a month I went to court and took a plea bargain. I was so ashamed of myself. Initially I was placed on psychiatric watch. I knew that with my recent history my family was worried that I would attempt to take my life. What they didn't know is that after walking out of that barn without a scratch except for where I had cut my arm, I was thoroughly convinced that God did not want me. I was not going to try to commit suicide and would never make another attempt. I would spend about six months in the county jail. After which I was going to prison for eight years.

The American

I spent four years and six weeks at Westfield Correctional Facility near Gary Indiana. When we arrived, I was surprised that it looked more like a college campus than a prison. The Indiana Reformatory, a medieval looking structure that was built in the 1850s, where some inmates were dropped off during the bus ride from the processing center was what I was expecting. Westfield, I would find out later had begun as a mental health facility, before evolving into a prison for the criminally insane. With the explosion in the prison population during the eighties Westfield had become one of the most dangerous prisons in the state. My final year there it was reported that Westfield had more incidents of assault on both officers and inmates than both the big prisons Indiana State, and Indiana Reformatory.

Amongst some White inmates throughout the state Westfield was known as a "Black" prison due to its population being forty-nine percent Black. Many inmates White, and Black, referred to Westfield as "The Thunder Dome" after the popular "Mad Max" movie sequel, as testimony to its reputation for violence. The day I arrived there was a stabbing in the tunnels. Because of my little jogging event the morning I was arrested I was deemed a flight risk and was housed in the Maximum-Security side of the prison. We were referred to as "Tunnel Rats"

Anthony Belcher

because all inmate moment was underground. During my time there I witnessed many stabbings and beatings. Gang members in my dorm rioted against the prison guards and took over the dorm effectively holding the rest of us as hostage. They beat up two guards and a sergeant pretty bad before the goon squad came in with ax handles followed by a Captain who fired one round of his M1 rifle to restore order. Between the rioting and the fighting and stabbing I read books, worked out, and wrote poems. I played basketball and smoked a lot of weed. I worked with a Clinical Therapist... When I left after four years I was just as fucked up as I was when I got there.

Pops picked me up from the prison on the day I was released, and we drove back to Ft. Wayne. It was January and cold outside. I didn't have a proper winter coat, so our first stop was the mall. As we entered the mall, I immediately began to feel uneasy. In prion finding yourself in the middle of a crowd, in many cases meant you were about to be stabbed. There was a specific incident that occurred one day while we were lined up waiting to get into the chow hall. We were fed by dorms and while one dorm was leaving another was on its way in. The tunnels were really narrow and there was barely enough space for a CO to walk down the middle. All of a sudden, we hear a scream and then a cuss

The American

and then a guy falls out of line with a shank sticking out of his abdomen. Complete chaos followed with guards and inmates fighting and the rest of us being rushed into the chow hall. These types of situations happened on more than one occasion while I was at Westfield. It would be many years before I would be comfortable being in crowded places.

The mall was full that day and I was surrounded by the comings and goings of the various shoppers. I couldn't keep my eye on everyone and even caught myself turning around in a complete circle while trying to watch everyone. By the time I picked out and purchased a coat I felt a full anxiety attack coming on. When Pops wanted stop in a music store and pick up a new keyboard, I had to come outside of the store and place my back against the display window so that I could make sure I could see everyone approaching me. For many years after I got cleaned up, I still wasn't comfortable in crowds.

When I walked into my mom's house for the first time after four years, my daughter Tonisha was sitting at the dining room table holding my daughter Danielle in her lap. Tonisha was now nineteen and had grown into a beautiful young lady. Dannielle was only three months old when I went away and was now a

Anthony Belcher

precocious four-year-old. I hugged and kissed them both on the cheek and cried like a baby. I cried even harder when Mom and I picked up TJ, my son Anthony Jr. from the fast-food restaurant he was now working. Anthony, who was about twelve years old when I left and only stood about waist high to me was now sixteen and looking me in my eye. My son had grown into a man, and I was not there to guide him.

Throughout my time in prison, I had not thought about my kids continuing to grow up while I was away. Though I was aware that they would not be the same little kids they were when I had left, I was not prepared for the reality that they were now young adults. My oldest daughter Corvetta had gotten married and had a daughter of her own. She and her husband actually lived in the same apartment complex where I would be living with my older sister Cindy. I cried again when I met her husband and held little Karissa in my arms. That night I went to bed realizing that I had lost something very valuable with my kids. Something I couldn't replace and would always regret losing.

Queen Esther and I had divorced about two years into my prison sentence. We met and talked about possibly making another go at our marriage. I wasn't sure what I wanted to do at

THE AMERICAN

the time. I wasn't sure if I was finished with drugs. I was certain that I didn't want to cause her any more pain. I told her that I needed to move on. I was able to get on as a cook at a restaurant within walking distance of home within the first month of being home. I was discharged from parole after six months. I started using again shortly after. There was plenty of overtime available at work and I fell into the pattern of working long hours during the week and spending my weekends smoking crack. I would leave Ft. Wayne after being home for a little over a year. In my mind my problems with crack and everything else all began and ended with Ft. Wayne. If I could go somewhere else, I could make a fresh start and leave the misery that was Ft. Wayne behind me.

I would later learn that this way of thinking was typical for an addict and was known as a "Geographical Cure". They are talked about at length in recovery circles because almost every addict blamed their location for their addiction problems at one point or another during active addiction only to find out that changing locations rarely worked. Still, I took off for Alabama hoping to get a job save some money and the move on to LA to try and restart my acting career. At least this is what I told myself. The truth that I wasn't saying out loud is that I was just running. Only I was running from me, not realizing at the time that no

Anthony Belcher

matter where I ran to or how far I was always going to find me at the end. Years would pass by before I figured that one out.

I arrived in the South with all of the preconditioned ideas held by many northern Blacks folk about that part of the United States. In my mind all Whites in the South were the people I saw on the evening news as a boy. Those pale white faces twisted with hatred and screaming vileness at Black folks many of them children seared into my brain. I was lucky enough to not encounter any of these folks during my time in Alabama.

As kids while Mom and Dad were together, we didn't get to visit Grandma and Grandpa Belcher who lived in Alabama. For whatever the reasons we, my brothers, and sisters and I were never allowed to join our cousins on the annual summer trip to spend with our grandparents. We were never told why she didn't want us to go, but I suspect she was concerned one or both my Grandparents would bring up the circumstances of my birth. I can't say for sure, however, I always felt that Grandpa Belcher had a problem with really accepting me as his grandson. I know now that some of Dad's family felt that Mom tricked Dad into marrying her. By the time I moved to the South in the mid-nineties both my grandma and Grandpa Belcher had passed on. I moved in with my

The American

uncle Larry on a little farm outside of Calera Alabama owned by my Aunt Gladys. She and her husband lived on a different property in a town a few miles away. Dad lived with a girlfriend on the other end of town, and Aunt Alberta and her husband lived in another little town, which was also only a miles away. Of course, all of them were aware of my troubles with crack, and all were willing to help me to get off the shit and get my life together. I was with people who loved me. I was with family. I found a job at a fast-food restaurant as a cook and soon was promoted to manager. It wouldn't be long before I was back to my old routine of working long hours and spending my weekends smoking. As also was my pattern once I became manager my end of shift receipts did not always make it to the bank.

Dad and I by this time had as good as a relationship as we could considering our circumstances. He had been sober now for close to twenty years and sort of evolved into an everything man for everyone. I suspect that in all working-class neighborhoods and especially in the Projects there is that one guy all the single women call on when they needed something fixed or attended to. That was Dad. I had no problems compartmentalizing my situation with Pops and Dad. Howard Gaulden was my biological father and had become the father figure in my life. Dad was my daddy. The

Anthony Belcher

daddy who's love little Tony Belcher wanted so desperately. We would never become friends; however, I did treat him with the respect due a father.

There were a couple of situations that stand out to me now from that time. One occurred while I was in the middle of a binge. I came to Dad to get some money back that I had given him to hold for me. It was late and I must have looked pretty desperate and pitiful. I was not being disrespectful to Dad but was refusing to leave until he gave me my money back. He began to cry and pleaded with me to go home and get some sleep promising to come and take me to get some help tomorrow. While all his pleading is going on I all of a sudden, I thought "Wow" the tides have turned. Instead of me crying and pleading with him not to hit me again, or not to hit mommy again, here he is crying and pleading in front of me. In my head the hurt little boy said with a coldness I have never felt prior to or since, I heard in my head, "How's It Feel Motha Fucka!" With a cold calmness I stood over him and wondered if he felt as helpless and fearful as I did back when I was a little boy begging and pleading with him. He finally gave me the money and I went back to my binge thinking every now and again life offers a little justice. Later when I began my own recovery process, I would make amends to Dad for that night.

The American

Another time I disappeared for about a week. I was hanging out in North Birmingham at a truck stop with some pretty shady characters. I had run out of money and capers and called Dad to come and pick me up. He was there in a flash and during the drive back to the farm the little boy in my head smiled because his daddy had come to rescue him.

For years I believed that my destiny was to be found in California, specifically the Los Angeles area. On the surface I believed that I would take another shot at making an acting career for myself. Underneath the surface I wanted to smoke some LA crack. In my soul I believed that whatever was meant to happen to and for me was going to happen in LA. I arrived in Long Beach California in early April of 1996 having been in Alabama for one month shy of a year.

I moved in with a friend from the eighties who lived in Pasadena. I picked up a job setting up appointments for an insurance agent specializing in insuring small businesses. It wasn't long before I was back to smoking and after about a year of being late to work and coming up short on my part of the bills both my employer and my roommate had had enough, and I moved back to Long Beach. I stayed with my brother William for

Anthony Belcher

a short while until he moved in with his girlfriend. I began living out of my car while making a few bucks here and there by landing the occasional job as a background actor on hit shows of the time "ER" and "Friends". Eventually, the car needed maintenance and through "crackhead logic" I decided it was better to sell it for a hundred bucks instead of getting it fixed.

That move pretty much ended the extra work and severed my last connection to legitimate society. I was in the streets. I needed to find a way to make some money. I tried "Pan Handling", realizing after only a few attempts that it really didn't work for me. I grew up in the projects and the mantra that "it was better to be a thief than a beggar", was a principle that had been driven into my mind since I was a young boy. So, I became a thief. I first tried armed robbery.

I was terrible at it. I went into a place once with my finger in my pocket and handed a note to the manager. The note said something to the effect that I had a gun, and this was a robbery. He demanded to see the gun calling my bluff and when I couldn't produce it chased me out of the store and down the block. There was another time when I actually had a gun. When I brandished it at the young counter person she began to panic, and I put the gun

The American

down and comforted her. I did get away with the money, however I ran away from the place with the gun still cocked. It's a wonder I didn't shoot myself. As the old saying goes "God takes care of fools and babies", and I couldn't have been a bigger fool.

For food I had would go into the large grocery stores and steal prepackaged sandwiches and the like to supplement my meals. It was during one of these trips that I got the idea for what would become my modus operandi. I ran into one of the women I knew who was also homeless. As I was entering the store she was leaving. She had completed her dinner heist for the night and as we passed each other, she held up the store bag she was carrying and asked me do you have your bag? I was confused by the question and wanting to stay focused on the mission at hand I nodded, waved, and kept going. It wasn't until later that it dawned on me that with the way these super grocers were set up, I could walk in fill up a bag or two with various items and then simply walk out of the store as if I had paid. Most of the time the alarms at the front either were not activated or did not work. I timed my "store runs" as I would call them, so that I was in the store during their peak hours. Using the crowded condition of the store as cover, I would bag up six half gallons of liquor, (back then grocery stores had liquor on the shelf), and then fill a bag with expensive choice cuts of steak and chicken. I would then roll my basket around the end of the cashier's isle and blend in with people exiting the store. I set up a regular customer base consisting of small business owners who bought the meat for half price and the liquor for ten bucks apiece. My take for these runs was on average around three hundred bucks. I would pay my driver his third, then we would buy drugs and rent a room. My first run occurred between eight and nine am in the morning catching the early shoppers. I would do it all again around five o'clock when the stores would be busy with the people shopping on their way home from work.

I chose shoplifting, ("Bosting" being the street term) because it was something, I could do alone, and it provided the least chance that someone could get hurt. By this time in my crackhead career, I realized that my previous endeavors at armed robbery could have gone really badly, and that it was only by the grace of God, or just plain dumb luck, I hadn't really hurt somebody. I was terrified by the thought of what could have happened during my foolish attempts at armed robbery and swore that I would not do anything where I had to use threats or violence again.

I was now literally homeless and a full-time everyday

THE AMERICAN

crackhead. I wasn't angry at my parents. I wasn't angry about my situation. I just wanted to smoke crack. I had convinced myself that I was a businessman. I wore slacks and a blazer. I had shops and bars as regular customers. Or I could go down to the docks and sell my goods there. For the most part I had a pretty good time for about ten months. However, as crackheads will do, I began to get sloppy. There was the time when I had got caught on a Saturday. The store instead of just chasing me out called the police. Because I didn't have any warrants and this was my first time getting caught in this area, the officer decided to give me a ticket for shoplifting and let me go. When I got caught the very next day at a different store in a different division, this officer too decided he was going to give me a ticket until he searched me and found the ticket, I had received from the officer the day before still in my pocket! That cost me a trip to the county jail. This became a pattern in which I would be caught, get a ticket and notice to appear in court. I had no intention of showing up to court and it wasn't long before those tickets turned to warrants. Eventually I knew that if I were caught, I was going to jail because of the warrants as well as the new charge. Still, it was just shoplifting and with the overcrowding issues in the LA County Jail system, a ninety-day sentence meant that I would actually

Anthony Belcher

serve not much more than a week or two. I usually spent those days in jail catching up on sleeping and eating as I didn't do much of either when I was on the streets.

One night I had just walked out of the store with six half gallons of liquor. It was a late-night run. and I am walking fast, causing the bags to sway and the bottles to clink as I make my way through the parking lot. I notice this little lady watching me and walking toward me. I had no idea what she could want. I knew she didn't come from inside the store, so she wasn't after me, however she kept coming toward me with this weird smile. Finally, she calls out to me asking if I am okay. I nodded that I was, smiled politely and tried to keep moving. She then said to me "You have a beautiful smile, but you are not happy. I can help with that." Her remark sent a chill up my spine, but I kept walking. I didn't know if she was crazy, a psychic, or just lucky but what she said to me was true. I was not happy.

I would go on and there would be more late-night runs which is totally a desperate act as the fewer people in the store made it a lot easier for Loss Prevention to spot the guy standing in the isle bagging up half gallons of liquor. Most stores were by then on the lookout for me as I hit the same three or four

The American

stores a couple of times a day. I had also gotten pretty cocky and began to believe my own bullshit. I believed that if I didn't act like I was doing anything wrong I wasn't doing anything wrong. I would leave the store pushing a cart put the bags in the car and often return the cart. One of the guys I hung out with use to tease me telling me I thought I was a ghost. As it turns out I was a bad ghost and an even worse lawyer as I was about to talk myself out of a six-month county jail term into a two-year prison term.

I had gotten popped again and figured I could use the weeks' worth of sleep and regular meals that would come with my ninety-day sentence. When the Public Defender came to the holding cell and informed me that they were offering me six months which would include the charge I had in Hawthorne I told him that I had already served the time for the charge in Hawthorn. I don't really remember what he or I said next exactly, but we argued, and he stormed out of the holding area. When he came back, he told me the prosecutor was now going to include a case I had in Indiana and give me a strike. His offer now was now two years in state prison. My case did not really fit the criteria for California's "Three Strikes Law" which had been recently come into effect. I had not committed a violent crime. It was obviously an abuse of the intent of the law, as stated when it was presented

Anthony Belcher

to the public. The law had been put on the books back in the early nineties and was intended to punish serious and violent offenders. I had neither committed a serious or violent crime in California. I would spend the next nineteen months at Avenal State Prison.

One of the classes I really enjoyed during my short college career was writing. I remember feeling my happiest when I received an A for review, I had written about that year's production of the play "The Elephant Man". It was during first prison term in Indiana that I began writing in earnest. I wrote a couple of scrips, (really bad), a few editorials, one after the LA riots of 1992 that was pretty good and was printed in Frost Illustrated, Ft. Wayne's black newspaper. I wrote poems, plays, I wrote almost as much as I read, and I was knocking off a couple of novels a week. All of my jobs in prison were of the office clerk variety, usually in the prison's educational apparatus, giving me access to computers and books. This access, at least when I was at Westfield sparked my creative juices. When I arrived at Avenal, I figured at the very least I would be able to use the time to get better at writing. However, I found out that I couldn't write. I tried daily to write a poem, a joke, something, anything only to come up with nothing. I did manage to write one poem and I share it here because it says exactly what I felt about my life and my future at the time. It's

The American

called

"Contemplations"

What a life

My life

No sugar no spice

Nothing good nothing nice

Lift me up, Let me down

Pick myself up off the ground

Turn around I'm down again

I want to stop but don't know how to begin

So I lift my head to the sky

And ask the Gods the reasons why

While I wait the earth don't shake

So I turn away...

And in hell I begin another day

Belcher 05

Throughout the time I was in the streets I still made sporadic contact with my family both in LA and back in Ft. Wayne. I had run into my brother William on the train a couple of times, and when I had my little car, my cousin Alex Datcher got me some extra work on her show "Goode Behavior". For the almost nineteen months I was at Avenal my family had no idea where I

Anthony Belcher

was or what had happened. I did not call anyone. I did not write any letters. I was pissed off. I was about three weeks short of parole when to my surprise I received a letter. It was from my baby sister Tracy pleading with me to let them know I was okay. She went on to write that she had been looking for me for about a year. The shame hit me hard, and I wrote her back letting her know that I was okay, and that I would be released soon. I promised her that I would contact Mom when I got out and that they shouldn't worry because I had learned my lesson and things were going to be different with my life. I gave the letter to the CO, (Correctional Officer), to mail out. I lay in my bunk that night thinking that what I wrote to my sister was all a lie. I was released in early February of nineteen ninety-nine. I went straight to the "Junk Yard", a notorious open drug bizarre located in an actual salvage yard located between the cities of Long Beach, and Wilmington California. By the end of my first night out of prison, I was back to boosting. By the middle of March of that year I was back in jail and on my way back to prison. This time I would get three years and would be sent to Corcoran State Prison one of the state's largest and home to some of California's most notorious felons. I had been out all of forty-five days.

When I look back at my stay at Corcoran today, I realize

The American

that going to Corcoran changed the trajectory of my life. One of the benefits, if I can dare call it that, of fully surrendering to my addiction was that somewhere deep inside my soul I knew that there was another life for me, that I would not always be a crackhead. I didn't know when, where, or how the change would come but as Sam Cook put it so eloquently "I know a change gone come".

With the number of celebrity actors and other famous folks in California being given prison sentences for possession and use of small quantities of drugs during the mid to late nineties, it became important that some form of drug treatment be provided by the Prison system to inmates with drug offenses and no violent crimes. What they came up with was the Substance Abuse Program, SAP for short. Two of Corcoran's lower level "yards" were turned into drug programs complete with counselors, classes, 12 step meetings and graduations as staples of the program. The two yards chosen, would not be subject to overcrowding and gang politics were downplayed. Each yard contained three buildings and each building contained two sections called "Pods". The Cos (Correctional Officers" were station between the two Pods. The "Pods" were all run by counselors. The COs were discouraged from entering the Pods unless it was strictly for prison functions

Anthony Belcher

like count, drug testing and emergencies. The two yards dedicated to the SAP program were run by the Phoenix House and Walden House Behavioral Modification programs. I was sent to the Phoenix House yard and upon arrival realized that this place was going to be something different. This environment was like no other prison I had been to and by this time if you count my sixth month stay in Pennsylvania, I was working on my fourth prison in three states. What Corcoran provided was an atmosphere where men were told they could change their lives. What Corcoran provided when I arrived there in May of two thousand one, was hope. "A change gone come"

They stood in front of us and shared their experience. They shared how they overcame growing up poor. They shared how they overcame growing up in drug invested neighborhoods where crime is considered a means of survival more so than a sin. These men with company badges pinned to their chests with titles on them like Manager, Vice President, Counselor grabbed my attention like no other group had before. The majority of these men were Black and Brown men of color, with a few hip looking White dudes thrown in. The authenticity of their experiences was evident in the way they spoke, how they dressed, and what they shared. I knew these brothers. I had served in the military with these brothers. I had gotten high with these brothers. These brothers were me. I knew in my heart that I was destined to be them one day.

Over the next two years I would rise the position of inmate counselor and be considered one of the best counselors on the yard, staff, or inmate. I became part of the crew of inmates who were charged with selling the program to new inmates just arriving on the yard. This was accomplished the thirty days new inmates would spend in our Pod. There were classes, seminars and groups inmates had to complete. At the end of their thirty days there was a big graduation ceremony for those just completing their thirty days. The effect this had on inmates was amazing to witness. For many of the young inmates, this graduation ceremony would be the first they had been a part of.

The debate goes on regarding the effectiveness of these types of prison programs and their success or failure. As a first-hand witness to the genuine joy of these inmates, some well into their forties, when walked up to the podium and received their graduation certificates, I can say that it did make a difference in how those men thought of themselves.

When I went through the prison SAP program I and a few

Anthony Belcher

others were provided with the tools we would need to go on to have successful careers in substance abuse counseling. The effect this environment had on me creatively has been unmatched since. It would be during this prison term that I would write more than I read. I would even perform a rap I wrote for one of the graduation ceremonies. These programs also offered what they called "After Care". Not only would you get drug treatment while in prison in a nurturing and supportive environment, once you paroled you would go into a 90-day program and once that was completed you would be provided 90 days of free housing in a sober living facility.

I would leave Corcoran after twenty-five months and move to the most beautiful location I had ever seen up to that point in my life. I was going to be living in a program whose front doorstep was on the boardwalk of Venice Beach!

Phoenix House was started in 1967, by six heroin addicts who came together at a detoxification program in a New York hospital. They talked about the struggles of staying clean and decided to help one another through the tough days ahead. Together, they moved into a brownstone on Manhattan's West Side and lived as a community, encouraging, and helping each other

THE AMERICAN

to stay sober. That is how Phoenix House was born. What made it work was the structure and approach to treatment brought to the program by psychiatrist Mitchell S. Rosenthal, M.D., and counselors from New York City's Addiction Services Agency.

In 1979, Phoenix House expands to the west coast and is gifted a property on Fruit Street in Santa Ana and opens its first residential substance abuse treatment center in California. In 1986, a second residential treatment center is opened on Ocean Front Walk in Venice Beach. (phoenixhouseca.org)

Most if not all drug programs of the time applied the principles established by Synanon (Synanon was initially a drug rehabilitation program founded by Charles E. "Chuck" Dederich Sr., (1913-1997) in 1958 in Santa Monica, California. By the early 1960s, Synanon became an alternative community centered on group truth-telling sessions that came to be known as the "Synanon Game". wikipedia.org)

The "Game" as it was referred to, is the staple of "Attack Therapy", a type of psychotherapy evolved from ventilation therapy. It involves highly confrontational interaction between the patient and a therapist, or between the patient and fellow patients during group therapy, in which the patient may be

Anthony Belcher

verbally abused, denounced, or humiliated by the therapist or other members of the group. During the seventies and especially the eighties with the crack epidemic in rage and the beginnings of the methamphetamine epidemic taking off, these types of programs became popular due to their being able to produce people who were able to maintain long term sobriety. Building on Bill Wilson's proven theory that the power of on Alcoholic working with another Alcoholic in keeping each other sober was unmatched. First with Synanon, and later Phoenix House and all of them like took this concept one step further and created the "Community', or "Family'. The idea being that addicts needed the community/family to love us when we were down. Tell us the truth when we were wrong and love us when we felt no one else did. I bought into these concepts hook line and sinker. All but one. It would be my unwillingness to comply with that one principle that would trip me up and send me back to prison one more time.

I arrived at Phoenix House that evening, right around dusk. I was amazed at how long I had lived in Southern California and never had seen the sun set over the ocean. It was one of those perfect LA nights and I stood mesmerized as the bright orange sun seemed to slip into the ocean turning the sky and the water a fiery mixture of red, orange, yellow, and blue. It was

The American

spectacularly beautiful. The next morning, I was up early and sat in the conference room looking out at the Pacific Ocean. I met with my counselor a no-nonsense Black woman around my age her name was Rochelle. We bumped heads almost immediately. I was given a job at the front desk, which in most programs is a real headache and this particular night I had a guy out front really acting out.

Rochelle was the only staff on that night and had been in group for a good amount of time. I became impatient after the guy in the lobby acted really belligerent toward me and barged into the group to get Rochelle. She kicked me out of the room immediately then closed it down. After dealing with the guy in the lobby she lit into me.

I defended myself saying that she didn't leave me any choice but to interrupt her group and her responsibility was not just her group but the smooth running of the house. I had a situation that she needed to deal with, and she should have dealt with it I told her. The back and forth escalated to the point where she actually told me I had to leave the program. Leave? For a moment I panicked. I couldn't leave, I had nowhere to go except back to the life that led me here in the first place, I couldn't leave.

Anthony Belcher

I looked at her and said while shaking my head no, "I ain't going nowhere"!

She looked at me for a second and said sit on the bench, which I did, then she walked away heading to her office which was upstairs. She was "shamming" me by sitting me in the front of the lobby on the bench which was commonly referred to by the residents as the "dunce" chair. If my memory serves me there was even a big white Dunce Cap sitting in the corner. Shamming, Learning Experiences, were tools used by the community to modify behavior. LE's often consisted of scrubbing the base boards and the floors with a toothbrush and a sponge. LE's, (learning experiences), were for the most part saved for family members who had experienced a relapse. I wasn't given an LE that night. Rochelle left me on the bench for about six hours until the end of her shift.

As Rochelle was leaving for the night, she told me to go to bed. I went to bed that night feeling good about myself even though my narrow ass was a little sore from sitting on that hard wooden bench for that length of time. It didn't matter. I felt good because I didn't quit. I didn't feel good because I didn't quit the pro9gram. I felt good because for the first time that I could remember, I didn't

The American

quit on me.

I met Lisa while we were both residents at Phoenix House. We began an affair while still residents and continued after we moved into our respective sober livings. Things went well for about a month. We sat together in horror as we watched the events of 9/11. We both got jobs doing phone sales. We went to meetings together and walked around Santa Monica and Venice basking in the sunshine. Unfortunately for me Lisa was a chronic relapse, and I was obsessed with her. It is recommended in all 12 step communities that people refrain from getting into serious relationships their first year of sobriety. In the therapeutic community romantic relationships between residents are as common as they are discouraged.

Lisa and I were the perfect storm of a couple. She was determined to be a victim and I was determined to save her. She would disappear and I would spend all my time trying to find her. She would show up, and I would help her to get into another program. Finally, I rented a room around the corner from the program she was last in, and she moved in with me. One morning we got on the bus together headed for work, we were working in different places by then, and her stop came before mine. We

Anthony Belcher

kissed said goodbye and I watched her walk down the street, not knowing that it would be for the last time. When I got home from work that night she was not there. Two more days passed, and I still had not heard from her. I eventually relapsed myself and soon after got arrested on a new charge. I would never see Lisa again.

I was back in jail on my way back to prison. I had been on the streets for about eight months. I was keenly aware that I had completely fucked up all that I had worked for since arriving at Corcoran almost three years prior. All of the cache I had established at Phoenix House was forgotten. My mind drifted back to the White kid at Corcoran who told me that a lot of folks was looking to see if I made it on the outs. They were counting on me. I remembered telling the counselor who checked me in at Phoenix House that my goal was to transition from my chair to his.

The miles went by, and I thought about how embarrassing it would be if they sent me back to Corcoran. While I realized that it might have been a good idea for me to have followed that one principle that I was adamant about not following regarding relationships.

The American

What baffled me was why I couldn't hear the warnings from my counselors and colleagues. They all could see that I was out of control with Lisa. Why didn't I see it? I had studied diligently the principles of the Therapeutic Community and was able to relay it to others with passion, earnestness, and authenticity. I was good at this. I was supposed to be the one that made it this time. This was not how I was supposed to end up.

For my fourth prison term I was sent to a facility in Northern California called CDCR in the town of Jamestown. CDCR are the Fire Camps of the California prison system. It is from these yards inmates are recruited to help fight California's wildfire season. Being sent to a Fire Camp is a big opportunity for inmates to stack up some money if they are deemed qualified. These guys are trained and then sent out to fires to assist the actual firefighters. At the time, the pay was something like a dollar an hour, however you were paid a dollar an hour for as long as you were in the field. Two weeks in the field and you would make yourself a couple of hundred bucks. When I first heard that I would be going there I thought hey, maybe the Gods have smiled upon me. Naturally, I was disqualified. The official reason for my disqualification was due to issues with my knees. I also believe that because I was forty-four at the time that age also played a part in their decision.

Anthony Belcher

I was given a job as a clerk in the GED educational program they offered. It was a good job, and the instructor was nice. My job was to assist inmates seeking to acquire their GED. The program was voluntary and in some rare cases court ordered. The classes were small, no more than five guys in each class. The classes were breaking up into two shifts leaving me to only have to work with two maybe three guys at a time. This left me a lot of time to mess around on the computer. I began to think about what other jobs I could possibly get when I paroled. I had access to a typing tutor program and using it taught myself to type. By the time I would leave I was very close to fifty words per minute. I figured I might be able to get a job as a "Data Processor" and thought that being able to type would be an important tool to have. While I didn't have internet access, it was still relatively new back then, I was exposed to lots and lots of information. One day while searching I stumbled across a form of Japanese poetry called "Haiku". The poems are structured using seventeen syllables, in three lines of five, seven, and five. I read that traditionally "Haikus" were meant to convey images of the natural world. I became obsessed with them and for about a month wrote a couple every day. Here is one of the first ones I wrote.

Teaching Tolerance

The American

Supports White supremacy
Why not teach respect.
BELCHER 05

Even with the discovery of Haikus I was not able to avoid the very intense self-reflection I subjected myself to nightly before finally being able to escape into sleep. One night while tossing and turning my mind ended up on my parents. I remember the old familiar anger sweeping over me as I thought about all of the years, of all of the lies and embarrassment. As I recalled the memories the anger grew. Then from nowhere I experienced what is referred to amongst 12 steppers as a "God Shot" and what is described in the "Big Book of Alcoholics Anonymous" as a "a moment of clarity". A quiet voice from somewhere deep in my conscientiousness broke through the cacophony of negative thoughts thundering through my mind and said "If your parents are so fucked up. Why do you keep going to jail? Everything stopped in my head. The noise had completely stopped, and as I fell into sleep the quiet voice kept repeating its question over and over again. If your parents are so fucked up, why do you keep going to jail.

When I arrived at Jamestown, I decided that I was going to read all of the books of the New Testament. Back during my time

Anthony Belcher

at Avenal, I had tried to get into Islam. I started to read the Koran and attended the prison Mosque for a couple of services. I looked into Buddhism. I was searching. God was at the top of my list of shit to be pissed off about and I had always thought of organized religion as a tool for the powerful to control the masses. At the same time, I was terribly uncomfortable with these feelings and new that I needed to make some sort of spiritual piece. I decided that Islam was way too restrictive for me. I began reading a Proverb a day and started to pray on occasion. Throughout it all I felt like I was just going through the motions. I really had no plan for what I was going to do once I was released. While I felt that I had armed myself with some skills, having learned my way around a computer and teaching myself to type, I knew that this time there would be no program picking me up at the gate. As I stood at the train station waiting to board for the trip south to LA I looked at my release papers which included orders to report to my parole agent within twenty-four hours. I threw the release paperwork into the trash and sat down to wait for the train. I had already made up my mind that when I arrived in LA, I was going straight to MacArthur Park.

I sat on the corner of PCH and Santa Fe Blvd. I was actually sitting on the curb. It was already a warm day. The sun was hazy

THE AMERICAN

that morning and I walked across the street to go to the little convenience store and steal my breakfast. I grabbed a honey bun and walked back across the street to Micky D's where I filled the large Micky D's cup, I kept with me just for these occasions. After filling my cup, I walked out of Micky D's and back across the street and resumed my seat on the curb. I thought about going back to the abandoned school bus I had been sleeping in for the past month or so but decided against it because it was already too hot to stay in there. I had been out of prison for about two and a half months. After a very short stay in the Salvation Army ARC program, I had been totally and completely homeless for the first time. I remembered the night I spent in Santa Monica walking aimlessly through the streets. I remembered pleading with the brother in the donut shop to let me have a couple of the stale donuts that he would be throwing away later that night. I thought about the time I had gone to the VA in Long Beach and told them I was suicidal thinking they would give me a bed. After meeting with the clinical person on duty they gave me a bus ticket and a sack lunch and sent me on my way. I thought about the many nights I spent walking up and down PCH all night because I had nowhere to sleep.

As I sat their sort of basking in the sunshine, that morning

Anthony Belcher

I began to think about how lucky I had been over the past couple of weeks. I reached into my pocket and pulled out the three "pipe" (possession of drug paraphernalia), tickets I had. This one particular White cop had popped me with a pipe on three different occasions but wouldn't arrest me. He had even confiscated my California ID and I would find out later mailed it to my Parole Officer. I thought about how I had missed my PO appointment by a couple of weeks, yet she still had not issued a warrant for my arrest. For a moment I thought Wow, things are actually going my way.

I finished off the Honey Bun and gurgled down the rest of the coke completing the process with a healthy burp. My mind began to drift to the needs of the day. I wasn't sure if I had filled out the paperwork to get my GR check and even if I had it wasn't due for another week, so I was broke. I thought about taking the change I had in my pocket and using it to catch the bus to the nearest grocery store and hitting a lick. I had found a few stores that had not yet switched over to the new security caps. As I was deciding which store was the closest and where I would go after to trade my goods for money. Everything seemed to stop moving around me, and I heard "If you don't get off the streets today you will be on your way back to prison tomorrow". The voice was so clear and matter of fact, that I got up and walked across the street to the pay phone and called my younger brother William who actually lived only about a ten-minute ride from where I was. William answered the phone and after saying hello, I asked him if he would come to pick me up. I was ready to go into treatment.

I sat with the counselor at the Clare Foundation in Santa Monica I felt pretty good about the thirty days I had spent in detox and was ready to be moved into the program outright. When the counselor began with Clare did not have the funding to accept me in the program my heart began to sink. The counselor went on saying that because you are a veteran you qualify for help from the Veterans Administration. She went on to say that the VA offered three different types of programs for you to choose from. She described the three programs as one being short and easy, one being short and hard, and the last being hard and long. Residential substance abuse programs back then were broken into basically three categories.

There was Detox and it normally lasted twenty-eight days. Short-Term programs were usually ninety days while long term programs required a minimum of a year commitment. The majority of Short-term programs used the Social Model approach

Anthony Belcher

which relied heavily on 12 step meetings and sponsorship. This approach was a lot different from the behavioral modification programs which relied heavenly on the Encounter Group, (attack therapy), and structured Therapeutic Community. The majority of these programs were considered as long 'term programs. I was well aware by this time in my life that the life I had been living for the past thirteen years or so was not who I was or who I wanted to live. I was determined that what I was able to do at Corcoran and Phoenix House was not an accident or a circumstance of chance. I was meant to become those men I had so admired when I first saw them in the Phoenix House prison program. I also realized that I was going to need a whole lot more than ninety days to get my shit together. I chose the long-term program and committed to doing a year in treatment.

    New Directions for Veterans is located on the sprawling West Los Angeles campus of the Veterans Administration. The entire VA complex is bordered by such high-end cities as Santa Monica, Culver City, and Century City and is literally next door to the UCLA campus. The grounds are green and well-manicured fronting fifties style buildings, giving it a look of nineteen fifties nostalgia. At the center of the complex is the West Los Angeles VA Medical Center, if not the largest VA hospital in the country

THE AMERICAN

it is certainly one of them. On the opposite side of the complex stands New Directions for Veterans housed in a long reddish colored brick building. Were you to enter New Directions back then, the first thing you notice are the mirror like shine on all of the floors. The front desk is manned by uniformed young men who are all neatly groomed. It feels like you have just entered a military installation.

The program was founded by two Vietnam Combat Veterans and a Social Worker from Santa Monica. Legend has it that John Keaveney, Larry Williams, and Toni Reinis broke into the then abandoned building designated VA 116. At the time it was flooded, filled with rats, and had electrical wires hanging from the ceiling. They enlisted the help of Congress Woman Maxine Watters, got themselves a grant or two and created New Directions Inc., a year-long, full-service program complete with its own dining facility, barber shop, employment center, and exercise gym.

The program promised that no veteran would leave there without fist achieving a year sobriety, a secure job or VA benefits and somewhere safe to live. The requirements for entering ND were at the time that you needed to be a veteran in good standing, homeless, and have drug and or alcohol addiction. Building 116

Anthony Belcher

was able to house one hundred and fifty veterans on the second and third floor. Also on the third floor was a separate twenty-four bed detox unit.

The program model was "Behavior Modification" administered within a "Therapeutic Community" using confrontational attack therapy as the standard method for addressing negative behavior. With the exception of John and Larry who both were graduates of the VA program all of the staff, from Program Manager down to attendants were all former graduates of the program. By the time I arrived they had opened another fifty-bed program in VA building 257 that specialized in treatment for Veterans who were dealing with both substance abuse and a mental health diagnosis.

The detox unit was a Social Model detox, meaning there were no nurses or doctors on staff, however, a VA nurse was assigned to the program to oversee that VA medication observation and recording protocols were met. The detox unit also functioned as a referral service that placed veterans in other VA programs or Community based programs, though the priority was to refer veterans to the two larger ND programs housed in buildings 116 and 257. The coordinator of detox during my time was

The American

a guy named Calvin. Monday through Friday he would assemble all the clients in detox into the day room for what was known as "Devotion", a combination informational, and motivational group. I was completely mesmerized by his authenticity and literally hung on to his every word for the three weeks I was there. I had decided that this time it was going to be different for me. I had come to that place that AA's Big Book describes as total and complete surrender. I realized that my best thinking had thus far resulted in my self-imposed estrangement from my family and loved ones, five prison terms in three states, and a crack habit that I did not want. I would do whatever they suggested, and I would do it the way they suggested.

I moved into the program proper on a Sunday night. The program held their big groups on Sunday and Thursday nights. The group was called "Family" and was where all the major business concerning resident phase movement, addressing negative behavior as well as highlighting positive behavior and accomplishments took place. The groups were led by the program staff. When Larry, Ricky, Dale, Willie B, Rene, Randolph, Carlton, and John Keaveney walked into group that first night, I sat there filled with the hope that I could one day be them. I experienced the same feelings as I did when I met the program staff of the

Anthony Belcher

Phoenix House prison program. These brothers were the real deal. They were former addicts, alcoholics, and crackheads who had all changed their lives.

Many had spent time in prison, and all had been homeless at one time or another during their using years. The Authenticity of their collective experience seemed to float around them like a cloudy shroud topped with a halo, leaving me feeling again that God was on my side this time. The program consisted of two phases. First phase focused primarily on getting an Alcoholics Anonymous, Narcotics Anonymous, or Cocaine Anonymous sponsor and completing the first four steps of the 12 steps as outlined in the AA Big Book. We were required to attend meetings in and around Santa Monica, and an on occasion we were taken to meetings held in South Central Los Angeles.

As in all behavioral modification programs, also known as "self-help" programs the residents do all the jobs in the "house". Every phase one resident is assigned to a work crew. The crews were responsible all of the business of the house. The Housekeeping crew was responsible for keeping the dorm areas, bathrooms, and floors clean. The Kitchen crew did all of the kitchen clean up and assisted in preparing meals. The Senior

THE AMERICAN

crew was responsible for running the front desk and policing the other residents. Phase one residents spent the majority of their day going to groups and working to keep the building clean and the nearly two hundred and fifty residents in the program fed. This pretty much made for a full day, and usually by no later than ten pm I would be fast asleep. I was initially assigned to the Kitchen Crew but after about three weeks I was made a Senior.

I felt like I was coming apart. Like I was walking around with my insides showing on the outside. I had never felt so vulnerable before then and have not since. I found understanding and solace in the AA Twelve and Twelve a book that focuses on explaining the Twelve Steps and Twelve Traditions. With this understanding I found hope and a freedom I had never before experienced. I began to realize that there were some experiences in my past that I had drawn conclusions about that were just wrong. The one that stands out the most was the time Mom had taken me to Harmer school in Ft. Wayne after we returned from England. I had to take a test so they could determine what grade to put me in. When the teacher was telling Mom how smart I was and she responded "My Tony" I perceived it as conformation that I wasn't good enough to be smart like Amos and Pam, instead of the genuine pleasant surprise Mom felt at hearing her child

Anthony Belcher

being complimented in that way. I was able to actually relive the scenario and see that I was wrong. While revelations of this sort were liberating to me because the more, I took an honest, sober look back at my life I began to see how my feelings about myself had controlled my thinking, and then controlled my actions. I was able to see how anger had been the driving emotion that shaped my perceptions throughout my life.

The book suggested I begin to take contrary action to my feelings. This was a technique used to achieve balance, by going against your initial reaction to a circumstance or person. So when I felt that the only sponsor that I could work with would be someone of the same race, same age, and similar experiences as me, I picked a guy who was ten years my younger than me, White middle class, and an Alcoholic. His name was Ryan. I met Ryan at an AA meeting where he was one of the people who shared his story. I liked his story and his general outlook on life. He also mentioned that he was a working actor, and I figured that made him the right choice for me. When I finally did approach him, I told him that I was not sure if he was the right guy for me, but I wondered if he would be my sponsor. He said he would, and we went to work on the twelve steps right away.

The American

Many people with addiction/alcoholic disorders have real problems with the 12-step process, especially with Step 4 which is the inventory step. The basic requirement of this step is admitting to another person the exact nature of your wrongs. I didn't have any real problems with the steps. I was clear about the things I did wrong and really didn't have any problems telling them to Ryan. Besides, I was certain that he or nobody else would judge me as harshly as I did. I was determined to complete all twelve of the steps and with Ryan's quiet, attentive manner and non-judgmental feedback, he helped me to learn a lot about myself and why and how I thought and felt the way I thought and felt. While this process proved to be somewhat healing it didn't provide the great breakthrough of insight and understanding into my psyche that I needed. In short, I didn't really feel any different about me and my life after completing the twelve-step process than I did before completing the process. However, the answers I was looking for were coming from a direction I would have never expected.

"Second Phase" was about employment and housing. In order to successfully graduate from ND one needed steady secure employment. Telemarketing and places like "Manpower" were not considered steady employment. The Employment Center was run

Anthony Belcher

by a lovely black woman named Bridget who, once she found a potential job for you, she would inspect your dress and coach you up before sending you out on the interview. Bridget and her staff were excellent at what they did and consistently placed former homeless veterans in, not only VA jobs, but jobs as diverse as Grey Hound bus drivers to cooks at Southwest University, and managers in some of the local grocery stores. Phase two residents were also eligible to work some of the paying jobs with the house. There were Resident Manager positions, Detox positions, as well as positions at the corporate desk. Once I completed phase one, I was hired as a Resident Manager.

Dale had been my First Phase case manager. Most of the residents assigned to him had either dropped out of the program within the first 90 days or stayed for the whole year and graduate. Usually when a resident made the transition from first to second phase, he would be assigned to a different case manager. It was pure coincidence that I would be transitioning to second phase at the same time Dale was promoted to second phase case manager. Dale was all drill sergeant with his approach to case management. I requested that I be allowed to keep him as my second phase case manager. Dale was a big man and was very intimidating. His aggressive confrontational style during encounter groups were

THE AMERICAN

legendary. I thought that he was a bully. I also thought that he was the most honest case manager ND had on staff. He was perfect for me.

Step eight of the twelve steps is the process of making amends to those you have wronged throughout your life. Both my daughters Corvetta and Tonisha were married and had children of their own. Corvetta or Peaches as we called her had a beautiful daughter named Karissa and a son named James. Tonisha had a son whose name was Deon. I had met Karissa when she was just a toddler, however I had been away in prison when Deon was born, and I had never seen him. As coincidence would have it, I was making my amends around Mother's Day. I decided I could send my daughters a Mother's Day card for the first time and in that card make my amends. At this time eight years had gone by since the last time I had seen them. While this process was going to be simple with Peaches, with Tonisha it was going to be a little more complicated. Tonisha and I had a falling out the last time I saw her, and I struck her, and she called the police. I spent a couple hours in jail and was assigned to some mandatory domestic violence classes. I never completed the classes and had to that point not spoken to Tonisha since the incident.

Anthony Belcher

There were two areas where I had the most difficulty. The first was in apologizing to Tonisha for striking her. I am from the old school and believed that kids who smart off to their parent's risk being popped in the mouth. Tonisha had spoken to me in a way that I felt was disrespectful and when I told her to be quiet, she would not. There was no reasonable person that I knew who would not support how I felt. I wanted to make amends for being a lousy dad when she was younger, but in no way felt that I needed to or would apologize for doing what any good parent would do.

What I failed to realize then was that in Tonisha's eyes I hadn't been a parent. However, Ryan in his way convinced me that I would benefit from doing making the amends, while reminding me that I had committed to working the twelve steps as they were written. Dale had said that it didn't matter how I felt, I should apologize for how I made her feel. Reluctantly I agreed and wrote on the inside of Tonisha's card that I was sorry for slapping her and mailed it off to her. It was the smartest thing I ever did.

I had got to where I only met with Dale when I had too. Part of this was by design as second phase residents were encouraged to depend on the work they did with their sponsor and engagement with the overall twelve-step community as

The American

guides on how to live a sober lifestyle. The idea was that you were setting up a support network for life after the program. I had grown tired of Dale and his hard-core style and communicated less and less with him about anything that was not concerning the program. When I got word from my mom that Tonisha had been trying to contact me I was surprised by how nervous I was at the prospect of talking to her again. I had no idea what I was going to say and was afraid that I might say something that would make the situation worse instead of better. I began to realize how desperately I wanted everything to be okay between us. The fact that she had called my mom and got the number to ND hinted that she might want the same thing. When I told Ryan about it, he suggested that I share this with Dale. I flat out refused to do so, and again he had to remind me of my commitment to do this the "Twelve-step" way and not my way, and once again I conceded to his wisdom. I made an appointment to meet with Dale. I had decided that I would also take this opportunity to tell him just how I felt about him. When I went into his little office that day, I had no idea that the great "emotional breakthrough" that I had felt had not happened for me was about to happen.

I let Dale have it as soon as I shut the door to his office behind me. I told him that I thought that he was a bully, and that

Anthony Belcher

he had never given me any credit for what I had accomplished in the program. He seemed surprised at my fury and actually asked me if I thought that he bullied me. That being his only interruption sat and listened patiently throughout my rant. I rambled on about some other insignificant issues before finally getting around to telling him about the Mother's Day card and the apology I had included in it. I told him that Tonisha had been trying to contact me and asked could I use the phone in his office to call her. He gave me that "I told you so" look as he handed me his cell phone and said, "call your baby man", he then walked out of his office closing the door behind him. I dialed the number and Tonisha answered the phone. After stumbling for a few seconds, I said "I am so, so sorry baby", and she said, "daddy I love you". From that point on I cannot really recall what was said between us, because I had completely broken down and was crying uncontrollably.

I was filled with shame, joy, and utter elation that I had not lost my daughters love. I cried unashamedly. We managed to end the call just as Dale walked up to the door. I gave him back his phone and went back to my job at the front desk. I cried throughout the remainder of my shift and pretty much through the night. The thought that kept running through my head was that if this child could still love me after the lousy father that I

The American

had been to her then I cannot possibly be the monster that I keep making myself out to be. The thought that followed was that I Have Been Wrong! I had been wrong about what I thought about me. I had been wrong about what I had thought about Dale. My perceptions were wrong, they were all based on my feeling that I was somehow responsible for the decisions and actions of my parents.

The tsunami of tears washed away all of the years of self-hatred and anger. The weight of it all washed away in the heaving uncontrollable sighs racking my body, and the burning tears running down my cheeks leaving me exhausted and drained. Finally finding sleep I woke up the next morning feeling fresh, feeling clean, somehow feeling brand new. I don't possess the clinical expertise to clearly explain why it was, that call with Tonisha that shattered my old belief system, however, what I can say is that from that point on I would address life differently from the way I had before. It was like I imagine someone who has had really bad cataracts removed from their eyes. I was seeing the world in a brand-new light.

Instead of approaching life from the perspective of "what is wrong with it' I was now approaching life from the perspective

Anthony Belcher

of "what is Right with it". I was learning to see the glass of life as being half full, instead of half empty. Where I once hated having to escort residents to the Arena League football games, I now was able to enjoy their joy which was displayed in loud and raucous cheering for the home team and jeering for the opponent. We had a group of guys who really loved these outings and though I never understood their excitement, I always considered the game as football in a gym, I recognized that because of my change in attitude, the nights I had to act as escort to these games were a lot more pleasant when I hadn't spent the entire night pissed off. My basic belief system had been changed. I now believed that as long as I put in an honest effort in any situation, I would always come out on the other side okay. I was no longer "waiting for the other shoe to drop", and the freedom I felt in my spirit was as refreshing as a summer breeze on a hot humid day.

    I had been placed in all of the leadership roles available in the program. While in first phase I was a "Senior Resident", when I moved up to second phase I was given a Resident Manager position and worked in detox. This progression was important to me because they were the positions I sought out because they were the positions that traditionally led to real employment within the agency. My goal after entering the program was to graduate

THE AMERICAN

and gain employment with the program. It was the first time that I had set a goal and then taken the right steps and made the right decisions to achieve that goal. My goal was to one day become a Case Manager. When I was offered a permanent position as a Detox Attendant, I knew I had achieved the first step in reaching my overall goal. I graduated from NDs residential program on a Wednesday and returned to work the very next day. I moved into a sober living facility that was run by a former ND staff member and located in Culver City not far from the Sony Movie Studio complex.

Making the transition from resident to employee was an easy one for me. I had already been working in Detox for my last few months in the program and the only difference from my perspective was that instead of going downstairs to the second floor to go to bed after my shift ended, I walked over to UCLA to catch the bus home to Culver City. I was renting a room and shared a kitchen with two other house mates. This would be the first time since arriving at Norton AFB that I would be living alone. It had been a long time since I had to worry about things like buying groceries and paying rent. I really felt good about my life. I had a job and keys to my own room, when only a year before I was sleeping in an abandoned bus and contemplating committing another crime. I went to work to meetings and back home. I hated riding the bus and as soon as I could afford to, I brought myself a car. It was a nineteen ninety SAAB, that I dubbed the "Blue Goose" due to its dark blue color. It was the first car I had purchased since the nineteen eighties.

I had begun to pay child support for Dannielle and was able to tell my mom that she could cancel the life insurance policy she had on me because I could now take care of these things myself. I was proud to finally be able to take care of my responsibilities. Standing up to these responsibilities made me feel like a man. However, it was the summons I received to appear for jury duty that gave me the greatest sense of pride and joy. I was surprised at how much joy receiving the summons gave me. it had been a long time since I consciously thought of myself as an American. I had never thought of being part of a jury or participating in any way in what is considered as an American's "Civic Duty". When I opened the envelope and read what was in it, I realized that receiving it meant I was being returned to a status that even I at the time hadn't realized how much it meant to me. I was an American citizen again!

I immediately began to make contact with my other

THE AMERICAN

children. Tonisha and I began to call each other at least a couple of times a month. I also was able to re-establish relationships with my son Anthony and my oldest daughter Peaches. Dannielle, my youngest was now in high school, and she and I spoke regularly. Many parents who are in early recovery have real difficulties with rebuilding relationships with their children after spending years in active addiction. Many relapses occur after some addicts develop unrealistic expectations about reuniting with their kids. The bulk of the credit for my being able to rebuild, and in Dani's case build from scratch, healthy, loving, and respectful relationships, goes to my children. I had to learn to allow them to take the lead in what our relationship was going to be. I understood, that especially for my older kids, who were all young adults now, that they no longer needed a "daddy". I realized that Dannielle really didn't know me at all. Today, I cherish our relationships and believe that in many ways they are more open and richer, than they would be if my kids had grown up in the house with me.

    Gary, my supervisor called me into his office and asked me to sit down. After I sat, he went on to tell me that he was going to be promoted to Program Manager of the ND Co-occurring Disorder program, and that he was recommending me to move up to Supervisor of the Detox unit. He went on to tell me that there

Anthony Belcher

were other candidates for the job, and that I needed to submit a resume to HR immediately. I'm not sure why but I really didn't take him seriously that day. A couple of days later he called me into his office and asked had I submitted my resume yet? When I told him I hadn't he again said to me that he thought I was the best fit for the job, and if I was interested, I needed to submit my resume that day. I complied and a week later I was called in and interviewed by our newly hired Program Director. Her name was Rachel, and she had come from a background of social work around LA and had worked for some of the larger agencies in the city. The interview went well, and I left feeling good about it but didn't think I would get the job, mostly because of the other more experienced candidates I was up against. I was on the bus heading home when I got her call informing me that I was the new Detox Supervisor. I hung up the phone and smiled. I had been out of the program and working as a Detox Attendant for all of six months. I thought again, God is on my side this time.

    I had no problem transitioning from Detox Attendant to Detox Supervisor. I had spent the six months, eight if you count the two months I worked while still a resident, learning every aspect of how the unit should run. With Calvin's assistance I learned how to navigate the HMIS system, (Homeless Management Information

The American

System), and had been performing intakes even before I became official staff. I had worked on all three shifts and knew the intake process and medication recording processes very well. Over the first few months I was able to hire on a couple of the guys who had been right behind me in the program and who had since graduated and began to build my team. As an attendant there had always been issues regarding policy and procedure. As I saw it my first job was to have a written policy for every procedure and task performed by detox employees. It took me only a couple of weeks before I had produced written step by step procedures for the intake process, recording medication intake process, as well as all of the general rules. I also created documents that were given to clients during intake providing them with a welcoming letter and documentation explaining to them what they could expect during their time in detox. I personally took over our referral apparatus and immediately increased the number of clients we referred to New Directions programs as well as other VA programs and programs in the outlying community. I developed relationships at all of the other VAs throughout the city and county, as well as Program Managers, and directors of some of the larger community-based programs. The unit was renamed the Assessment Center. I began to work more closely with the

Anthony Belcher

Outreach team, and when the supervisors position became vacant, I wrote a proposal to the Executive Staff making a case for why the Outreach team should be brought under the umbrella of the Assessment Center allowing me to supervise both. My proposal was granted, and the Assessment Center/Outreach Team was born.

The Iraq war had been going on now for about a year. Saddam Husain had been captured, tried, and hung. President Bush had declared the war over, the previous summer only to turn around and commit more troops to the region in the fall. There were protest outside of the White House, and on college campuses throughout the country. In big cities like Los Angeles, New York, DC, Seattle, protesters were in the streets.

America looked a lot to me like it did in the Sixties. There was but one significant difference in these modern-day protests when compared to those during the war in Vietnam. That difference was in how they treated American soldiers returning home from the war. Where soldiers of my generation were welcomed home from Vietnam with cries of "Murderer", or "Baby Killer", these veterans returning home from Iraq were treated as heroes. Though there was some animosity felt by the veterans

The American

of my day towards these newly returning veterans, overall, we were all happy that the American public finally understood that it was our politicians that were responsible for bad or immoral wars, and that our soldiers were the first victims of these wars. Many of these veterans were returning home with Post Traumatic Stress Disorder, (PTSD), known as "shell shocked" in my day, and were ending up on the streets.

Homelessness amongst soldiers returning home and veterans in particular had become national news. Los Angeles county boasted the largest population of homeless veterans in the country. The Executive team at New Directions were intent on being at the forefront of providing services to the growing number of homeless veterans about eleven thousand, which amounted to about ten percent of the entire LA County homeless population.

As the new manager of the Outreach team, I was now in many ways the face of the agency. I was assigned as the agency representative whenever there were meetings and seminars where all of the VA and community-based programs were in attendance. My team and I started to conduct "ride along" trips with the four major TV networks in Los Angeles. Soon we were doing this for journalist from magazines as popular as "Newsweek", to

Anthony Belcher

newspapers and magazines from countries like France, England, and Japan. I and my team my established a jail outreach program and I was allowed to enter not only the county jails. My goal was to spread the word about our twenty-four-detox giving the police officers the option of bringing an intoxicated veteran to us instead of to jail. I found that going into the jails as a free man was a little strange, but not terrible because I could walk back out when I wanted. However, when I was invited to and cleared by Corcoran State Prison to come to Phoenix House and share my story with the inmates, I was very proud of myself.

When I walked from the visiting center to the number two yard at Corcoran State Prison, the first thing, I saw that I recognized was the red metal sign with the white bold writing "Warning No Warning Shot". A shiver ran throughout my body as my mind grasped the reality that I was going back to prison. For a second, I began to walk with the stated shuffle of men wearing leg irons. It was only a second and then I was being greeting by all of the counselors whom I had spent a little over two years learning from as an inmate. I had been two years since I saw them all. We spent a really nice lunch together reminiscing about my time there and gossiping but inmates and counselors that we all knew. After lunch we walked a couple of laps around the

The American

prison yard. Following that same circle I had walked every day for two years. I got a chance to go up to my old cell and look into it before meeting with inmate's downstairs in the dayroom. Two years' worth of memories raced through my head. I was no longer the man who had lived in this cell.

That man was filled with doubt, low self-esteem, and had no direction or purpose for his life except maybe to destroy it. The man standing outside this cell now was a symbol hope. The man I was now, who would be speaking to the couple of hundred inmates that would be in attendance was walking living proof that they change their lives. They greeted me with applause. The enthusiastic applause of seeing one of their own do good. As I stood before them humbled by their welcome, I realized that I had achieved a goal I had set shortly after I walked into this building for the first time so many years before. The applause began to slowly fade, and I stood before them realizing that I had become the someone who could give these men hope. I was now one of the brothers who had so impressed me right here in the same spot, saying the same things they had said to me some five years before.

Even with the success I was experiencing at work, the

Anthony Belcher

voice in my head still muttered on, telling me that it wouldn't be long before I fucked this up too. There was a period during time in the first phase of the program where I was experiencing very real daydreams about smoking crack. Every night before I fell asleep, I would play the same scenario where I was smoking crack. I finally went to Dale about it because I was so afraid, I was headed for a relapse. After calming me down he reminded me that I had been smoking crack, and getting high a lot longer than the six months I had been sober. He went on to explain to me that my brain was used to thinking about crack, and creating get high fantasies. He then reminded me that I hadn't left the program to go get high, and that I had come to him to talk about what I was feeling. He went saying that in the past I would have never come to anybody about what I was feeling and would have eventually succumbed to the thoughts in my head. He told me that I could change how I thought when I learned to change how I talked to myself.

The official name for the little voice is "self-talk". The basic idea is that people like me have to learn to change our self-talk from negative to positive. With the end result being that we change how we feel, which automatically changes how we act. I began a little ritual to fight back these negative thoughts and

The American

feelings while still a resident in the program.

Every morning I when I woke, I would get up make a cup of coffee, and smoke cigarette. While enjoying my smoke and my cup of joe, I would read the corresponding Proverb for that day. I would then end my "quiet time" with the 23rd Psalm, which I had adopted and still is to this day my prayer, I say my amens and tell myself that "I deserve the best life I can have". Then I hit the shower get dressed and hit the good old 405, (four or five mile an hour), freeway and head to West LA and good old ND. This was literally how I began each day. For the first five years after graduating from the program I also attended an AA, NA, or CA meeting weekly. I had asked God to show me how to love. I asked God daily to help me to become a better man. I was now the type of man that I had always wanted to be but didn't know how to be for so many years of my life.

I was now a program manager for one of the largest programs in LA, and the country. I was respected by my supervisors, my peers, and my clients. I began to realize how long it had been since I had seen my family. I hadn't been to Ft. Wayne in over ten years. During that time, my sister Cindy had passed away from cancer. Both my uncles Howard and Gilbert

Anthony Belcher

had also passed away. These events happened during my prison years, and I was not able to attend any of their funerals. I had been with ND now for two years and had renewed my relationships with all of my kids and now spoke to them all regularly by phone. Over the past two years, Dani taught me how to instant message on yahoo messenger and we usually chatted a couple of times a week. Still, I hadn't seen her since she was six. Anthony was now in his twenties and had a five-year-old of his own. Peaches now had a son. Finally, my grandmother was in a nursing home suffering from full blown Dementia. It was time to go home.

I arrived in Ft. Wayne right before the fourth of July. I was surprised by the greeting given me by my family. I was being celebrated as if I had just returned from the moon. Now that I think about it, maybe from their perspective having a loved one lost in the abyss of cack addiction and prison, I had returned from the moon or worse. Dad, his new wife Stella, and my Aunts Gladys and Alberta came up from Alabama. Amos Jr. and his family all came to Ft. Wayne. Sheila had gone and picked up Dennis, who was now in his fifties.

We held a hastily put together family reunion in Rock Hill Park which was located in our old neighborhood, and I was able

The American

to see not only family but folks from the neighborhood came by as well. I had coordinated the trip so that I could be there for Dani's sixteen birthday. She was a high school basket baller and hit me up for a new pair of "Jordan's", after which I went by her house and showed her where she got her jump shot from. I had not really seen her older brothers and sisters since back in eighty-nine. Sonya, Michelle, Tamika, and Luon were all grown now. Luon was actually playing professional football in Germany, and I wouldn't see him, but I did get a chance to see the girls and make a personal amends to them.

All in all, the trip was wonderful. However, the love and admiration I felt from my family felt a little strange. Not strange as in unfamiliar, I had always been popular within the family. What felt strange to me was that I finally could believe that what they were saying to me was genuine. The little boy in my head that had always warned me not to trust these people was quiet.

I had asked Sheila to take me out to Cindy's gravesite. Me, Pam, and she dove to the cemetery and spent about fifteen minutes looking at the little plaque in the ground before I said to Sheila "My sister ain't here, let's go". I went there hoping to find some closure, but all I could feel was emptiness as I stood

Anthony Belcher

there looking down at the little plaque that marked the life of this woman who had meant so much to me.

My grief would come about a year later while watching "Sister Act II" starring Whoopie Goldberg, one of Cindy's favorite movies. I was sitting on the couch enjoying the movie one Saturday afternoon. One of the characters in the movie, a short bald-headed priest, did this little dance that used to crack Cindy up. When that scene came on I all of sudden could hear Cindy laughing which caused me to laugh too. Soon my laughter turned to tears and finally to full blown weeping. I cried consistently for a good ten minutes. But that day, that day I didn't feel anything. Mom, Sheila, and I went a few days later to visit Granny at the nursing home.

The Thelma Mae Ross I had grown up with was gone. Alzheimer's had pretty much taken over her mind, and she didn't remember me. Still, she was pleased to have company and had the sweetest of dispositions. I know her condition bothered Mom, who Granny kept calling Elsie, her older sister that had passed away years before, but I couldn't help but think that she was somehow free. In her present condition I thought that I was being given a glimpse of the girl she had been so many years ago. We

The American

spent a very pleasant afternoon with her before heading home. It was about a month after I returned to California that Mom called me and told me she had passed. I also spent time with Pops and his family, getting by to see his older brother Harold whom, we all called HL. He was in pretty poor health but recognized me when I came in with Pops. HL had been a grounds crew member for one of the Tuskegee Airmen squadrons that served in WWII. He was very proud of his service and kept a picture of him and his fellow crew members that had been taken during the war, next to his favorite armchair. He would pass on later that year, and I am glad I got to see him that last time. His passing hit Pops harder than he liked to let on, but I could tell how much it hurt him to lose him.

All in all, my trip home had been everything I had hoped it would be with one exception. I would not get to see Tonisha. Five more years would pass before I was able to fly to Atlanta and spend a lovely week with her son Dion and husband Damien. I rented a car and drove to Ft. Wayne with Dion as my co-pilot. It was a nice long drive with just me and my grandson.

I picked up the phone and answered with my usual, "This is Anthony Belcher, Thank you for calling New Directions, how can I help you", when I heard the voice on the other end say, "Hello

Anthony Belcher

Mr. Belcher this is Ms. Jones calling from the Pentagon, do you have a few minutes to speak to me?" I froze for a second and then held the receiver out so I could look at it. The Pentagon? I thought. What the hell did the Pentagon want with me? In real time I confirmed that I was me and listened with eyes widening as she explained that she was calling on behalf of Admiral Mullen, The Chairman of The Joint Chiefs of Staff.

Admiral Mullen had recently replaced Colin Powell in the position, and I was keenly aware that I was speaking to the office of the highest-ranking military officer in the whole US of A. The person on the other end of the phone went to explain that the Admiral had read about me and my team in one of the national magazines and was highly impressed with the work we were doing. She went on to say that the Admiral was really interested in hearing form me what he might be able to do to help our cause. It was then that she extended the Admiral personal invitation to me to come and visit him at the Pentagon! I explained to the lady that I was humbled by the invitation but would need to pass this on to our executive team to take care of the details. While the agency elected not to send me to DC, coincidently Admiral Mullen grew up in Orange County and would be traveling to the Los Angeles area the following year.

The American

ND laid out the carpet for Admiral Mullen and his entourage. It had been over thirty years since I had worn a military uniform but when I saw all that brass walking through the Assessment Center Doors I snapped to attention and saluted them as the filled into my little day room. Admiral Mullen and I seemed to hit it off and we spent about thirty minutes together while I explained what we did. He was genially interested in the wellbeing of the veterans who were going through various stages of detox and stopped for a few minutes at each of the twenty-four beds to give a word of encouragement. As I watched this very accomplished white-haired gentleman provide comfort to each of the former soldiers, airmen, marines, and sailors, some who had seen actual combat and some who had been living in the streets for the past twenty years, I thought that this is a man who understands and bears the responsibility for sending men into combat. The respect and genuine concern he and all of his entourage, all high-ranking officers themselves, left me feeling proud that I had served. Though I hadn't thought about it in these terms in more years than I could remember, as I stood watching these men treat these broken soldiers as they did made me proud to be an American.

When Dad died in the fall of 2008, I knew that I was not

Anthony Belcher

going to be able to make the trip to Alabama for the funeral services. I hated that I wasn't going to make it to the services and felt that because I didn't there would be members of the family who assumed I hadn't come because of Dad's and my past. The plain truth is that while I wasn't broken up about news of his death, I really wanted to be there to see him off and hang out with all of my cousins. Dad was the last of Belcher men to go and I would have liked to have been there to offer support to my two Aunts Gladys and Alberta. I was able to call to Calera and order a nice floral display to be placed on his coffin. The night, or day, I am not really sure which, but it seems that news like this comes more often in the night than the day. In any case, I lay in bed that night thinking, "Wow, ole Snoop is gone." Snoop was a nickname I heard a cousin of his call him that has always stuck out in my mind.

The fear and anger I had felt toward Dad had all been exercised with my completion of the twelve steps. We did not have a close relationship the four years I had been sober since graduating the program, however, I felt it was my duty so to speak, as his eldest son, to make sure I called him at least once a month. There were times I felt that I could and should have done more to try and bring us closer, however I was keenly aware that Dad

The American

would be just as happy acting is if the past had no effect on us at all. Still, I lie there that night remember the wonderful Christmas mornings, I thought about the time we were talking on the phone, and he was yelling at a rooster. I asked Dad, why is the rooster in the house? Dad replied that the rooster thought that it was his house. I said, Dad you might want to consider remarrying since you have gotten to a place in life where a rooster is running your house. Dad replied in his witty way that "no, if the rooster gets too far out of line, I can cut his head off and eat him. I'd be just stuck with a wife" I laughed until I cried thinking that now there is some wisdom for your ass.

I realize today that Dad and I had the relationship we had. It is what it is. I no longer think of him as a monster, and I understand and appreciate how the issue of me helped to fuel his alcoholism. That said, I would be less than honest to say that it hasn't taken me some years to get to where I am today emotionally in regard to my life with Dad took some time. I never had the conversations with Dad that would have given me better insight into what he was like as a young man. I miss not having those conversations with him. Today I am able to remember the good times with Dad as well as the bad. Today I remember that he was sober a lot longer than he was a drunk and he spent the

Anthony Belcher

majority of his life as a valued member of our family and the community at large. Today, I wish he rests in peace.

While my professional life was going very well, my personal life was pretty much a mess. For whatever the reasons I always seemed to be moving from one incompatible relationship into another with little or no break in between. Over the next five years I would be married and divorced twice. During one of these relationships, I would relapse after coming home from work to find my wife missing. I went looking and eventually found her in a motel in her old neighborhood getting high. I joined her and for the next six months we got high on the weekends. I realized that what we were doing is not what I wanted to do and walked into the apartment one day, handed her four hundred dollars and turned around and moved out. As is the case with all crack heads, things got out of hand. I had a no call no show for about half a day, and that was all that was needed to start the rumor mill.

The rumors became so prevalent that Rachel our Program Director, asked me to submit a urine sample because she had planned on putting me in a new position and she was under some pressure to address the rumors. I explained to her that one negative test was not going to quiet the rumor mill and volunteered to go on mandatory random testing for the next year. At her request I sent an email to both the Executive team and the Management team informing them of my decision. I had no real problem with not smoking cocaine. Simply put, I had absolutely no more desire to destroy my life, and that is what cocaine had been for me. I had absolutely no more need to punish me for my childhood, which is what smoking crack had been for me. I just stopped. I had no desire, no night sweats, no nothing, I just stopped.

    I was randomly tested for the next year with no problems. I was appointed as liaison between the program and clinical staff and was given the task of bringing the two departments together. Historically their different philosophies and approaches to recover often clashed. I had always worked closely with the clinical team as the Assessment Center Supervisor. I had coordinated with the clinical team for years to properly assess which program we offered was the best the fit for the veteran's needs. The relapse had forced me to look differently at the Therapeutic Community/ Behavioral Modification modality than I had before. Philosophies like "Harm Reduction" and "Housing First" looked at the process of recovery from the perspective of "What Happened to cause the bad behavior", as opposed to the "correcting the bad behavior".

Anthony Belcher

Relapsing and being able to walk away from it unscathed forced me to look at myself in a different light. It hadn't gone unnoticed by me that, whereas at one time a relapse would have led to the eventual collapse of whatever life I was living at the time, this time I would be able to use it to become better at my job.

I was at a company retreat when I got the call from Aunt Josephine that Pop's had fallen and broke his hip and had been taken to the Nursing Home because of his being in a confused state. She told me that I needed to come home and make some decisions about what he was going to happen to him next. I told her that I would be there as soon as I could arrange it with work. I called and talked to Pops later that night and ended up crying because he sounded weak and confused. I hung up the phone convinced that he was dying. While in Ft. Wayne I had noticed that Pops appeared to be a lot thinner than was normal. I chalked it up to the aging process and didn't think much else about it. Of course, he assured me that he was in good health and that the loss in weight was nothing for me to worry about. I now mentally kicked myself for not pressing the issue about his health with him while I was there. I made the arrangements to be off work and took the flight to Ft. Wayne.

THE AMERICAN

I was caught off guard at how small and weak Pops looked as he lay in his hospital bed. I could see that he had pretty much resigned himself to the idea that his time was near. The diagnosis was that he was in the beginning stages of Alzheimer's disease and could no longer live on his own. Pops had agreed to moving into the Nursing Home's assisted living facility. I went about the business of closing down his apartment. At his and Aunt Josie's insistence we went to the funeral home so they could explain to me how things were supposed to go. I really got emotional when Josie and I returned to Pops room and broke down in tears. It all felt so surreal to me. I couldn't really wrap my head around that my Pops may die soon. Then there was Mom.

Mom had always resented that I had gotten to know Pops and even more so that we had a close relationship. When I told her that Pop's may not have long to live, she asked if I was going to be named in his obituary. That was it! We were going to have it out. I, in a calm voice said to Mom that I was only acting like the man she had raised me to be. I went on to tell her that it was okay that Pops was my father. I told her that I was proud that I was Pops son. I told her that I was sorry if me acknowledging him made her feel bad, but it was my choice and that I would be less than the man she raised me to be if I didn't acknowledge him.

Anthony Belcher

Eventually she succumbed to my logic and when I came back to Ft. Wayne to pick up Pops two weeks later to come live with me in California, He, Mom, Me, some old friends of theirs, along with my daughter Dani and my sister Sheila, had a very nice dinner together the night before we left.

Pops loved LA and his health improved almost immediately. We enrolled him in the neighborhood Sr. Center, and he went there twice a week. He became a popular member among the older ladies, and it wasn't long before he had a girlfriend. Over the five years we were together he would have a different girlfriend for each year. Pops had gotten old, but he hadn't gotten "That" old! There were free jazz concerts on Fridays held at The Los Angeles County Museum of Art and Pops and I became frequent visitors., He began to play music again, even having me call back home to have the guitar he had left with a friend shipped to us here in LA.

We went to the beach. I took him to work with me on occasion when he had appointments at the hospital as ND was located on the same VA campus. He would sit there beaming with pride as clients and staff alike pampered him. Everything was going pretty well. Pops had pretty much recovered completely and was his old self again. He had had one cataract surgery and when

The American

I took him to the hospital for the second to be done, I expected the same routine of his being there for a couple of hours before I picked him up and we headed home. I went to get some lunch a few blocks away and had just finished eating when I got the call from the VA. that Pops had had a serious stroke.

He recovered but was never the same after. He began to have trouble with things like working locks and fastening buttons. I'm sure it didn't help that I was breaking up with my fourth wife. We moved into a two-bedroom apartment about two years after his arrival in LA. Pops continued with his routine of going to the Sr. Center a couple of times a week. I would fix his breakfast before I went to work in the morning and make dinner for him when I came home. After dinner we would watch a game and engage in long conversations. For a while, things were similar to the days when we first met, and we used to sit in his apartment in Ft. Wayne watch sports and discuss the world at large.

New Directions had completely transformed from the long-term residential program it was when I entered it back in two thousand three. John Keaveney and Toni Reinis, two of the three founders were no-longer a part of the agency. Rachel Feldstein, the Program Director was also gone. In their place as CEO was

Anthony Belcher

a young Black man named Gregory Scott. He appointed Richard Caines as Director of Programs. Richard, another Black man would be my boss. With the guidance of these two brothers and the excellent support staff they built ND became a program that not focused more on the clinical aspects of addition and providing permanent supportive housing for veterans who came through their programs as well as a referral service for veterans in the community. As part of a drive aimed at increasing our footprint on a national level, I was chosen by Mr. Scott to represent New Directions at a three-day conference for veteran's programs that was being held in Washington DC!

I stood looking through the iron fence that surrounds the White House hoping to get a peek and President Obama or one of his family. The fact that the President of the good old US of A was a Black man was not lost on me. In many ways I considered the election of our forty-fourth president as White Americans making a real amends for Slavery. I was amazed at the different races of people that flowed through the MLK monument and stood in awe of the beauty of the Jefferson and Washington memorials. The Vietnam War memorial held a special place in my conscience because it was the war I grew up with. I stood there in front of the Wall filled with the names of those who had sacrificed their lives

The American

for their country and saluted them. I was humbled by the marble floors and the power that seemed to emanate from the very walls of the US Capital building. But it was the Lincoln Memorial that was by far the most amazing to me. It attracted more visitors than all of the other monuments combined. I was duly impressed and feeling mighty patriotic by the end of that day. I was proud to be an American.

Pops could not stay at home by himself anymore. There had been a couple of days when I had to leave work because he couldn't figure out how to get his key to work in the door. Shortly after we had moved into our apartment I met, my now wife Yolanda. Her middle daughter Amber attended school in the evenings and did some babysitting for a friend during the day allowing her to be available to help out with Pops. She and Pops became fast friends, and she would come over daily and fix his meals and take him to the Sr. Center a couple of times a week.

The Alzheimer's was taking over, and more and more Pops was trying to get out of the house at night. I began to sleep in the living room and caught him trying to get out of the door on more than a couple of occasions. Finally, the worst happened. Pops got out of the house and was wondering off down the street. Yolanda

Anthony Belcher

was able to catch up to him, but he would not respond to her and just kept walking. She called me and I left work immediately. When I finally got home, I found them walking up the street back towards the house. Yolanda told me later that Pops had walked into the park and couldn't go any further because it was fenced in. We got him back into the house and that night I made peace with the reality that I could no longer take care of Pops and he needed to professional help. The next day I took him out to the VA hospital and left him there. I cried all the way home. Though his attitude toward me which had become contentious due to the advancement of the Alzheimer's, his overall health deteriorated fairly quickly. Pops died a few months later.

Yolanda and I had met at a grocery store and had pretty much lived together since. Neither of us at the time were thinking of marriage but seemed to coexist nicely and had now been together for about two years. Yolanda had graduated from Grambling University, as did her oldest daughter Ashely. Of course, Pops, having grown up in the town of Grambling, became instant fans of the whole family. Yolanda After Pops passing, Yolanda's fifteen-year-old daughter Destiny came to live with us, and I got the chance to be a father to a teenage girl. Destiny was on the cheerleading squad and participated in many other after school

THE AMERICAN

activities. I enjoyed picking her up from practice and attending all of the pre-collage activities she had attended.

This was all new to me and the enjoyment came with some guilt that I had not been around to be a part of my own daughters' teenage years. Both Dani and Tonisha have come out to California to visit, and today we are one big happy family. My sister Tracy who lives in Maryland near DC was getting married and Yolanda and I took Destiny with us so she could visit the campus of Howard University as it was one of the schools, she was considering attending. Destiny became the darling of my mom and her sister my Aunt Kay, who lived in Atlanta, and would be of big help in getting Destiny some financial assistance which all but secured her enrollment at Clarke Atlanta University. Destiny would choose Clarke, and Yolanda and I took off work for two weeks so we could go to Atlanta to get her enrolled. I remember talking to my sister Pam, who also lives in Atlanta about how wonderful it was to see so many young Black children going to college.

Though attending college could have been an option for both of when we were coming out of High School, we were keenly aware that the beauty of what we were seeing was the part of

Anthony Belcher

Black America that was missing from the American national conscience. While the "Cosby Show" and its spinoff "A Different World" had introduced all of America to the fact that Black people did go to college for something other than to play sports, watching those kids that day, Pam, and I both realized we were witnessing something special. The main reason Yolanda and I had taken so much time off work was so that I could take Yolanda and Destiny to Alabama to meet My Aunt's Gladys and Alberta who lived in Calera, and then to visit my brother Amos, who lived in Huntsville. We also spent some time in Monroe Louisiana which is a few miles from Grambling with Yolanda's daughter Ashely and her family. We spent time with my cousins Steve and his wife Taneal, who also lived in Atlanta before returning back to California. All in all, it was a wonderful trip.

    The trip highlighted for me just how important it was for me to be a part of a family. To be respected by that family and be someone that family could be proud of. Of all of the blessings I was able to finally recognize that God had bestowed on me was my family. I am very grateful for the relationships I have with my sons Anthony and James, as well as Yolanda's son Sean. I also have been blessed with three grandsons, James Jr., Anthony the third, Dion, and Liam. My granddaughters Karissa, Charlotte, Naomi

The American

and Liaysia are all beautiful and the apple of their grandfather's eye. Little did I know that I was about to be blessed again.

"Hello, is this Tony Belcher", yes, "My name is James Cannon, and they tell me you are my father", I held the phone away from my ear and looked at it. Is this really happening I thought. This call sounded almost exactly like the one I made around thirty-five years ago. I said, "Hi James", I have heard that too. The rumor that I had had another child while I was still married to Cheryl had been a thing for many years. I knew about James, and the possibility that he was my son. When I returned to Ft. Wayne from LA back in nineteen eighty-three James's mom, Vanessa, a very beautiful and sexy Black woman whom I had had a brief affair with back in nineteen seventy-seven had moved with him to Colorado. I had not seen or heard from either of them until that day in twenty twelve. Our conversation went very similar to the one I had with my Pops those many years ago, and I am happy to report that today we talk regularly.

Shortly after returning from our trip to Atlanta Mr. Scott was let go from New Directions. It wasn't long after that Richard Caines was also let go. When I was let go in December of that year, I wasn't surprised nor even angry. It was definitely

Anthony Belcher

inconvenient as Yolanda, and I were to be married that Christmas Eve. Their decision to let me go didn't affect our plans and we were married in a nice little Chapel with her family and a few friends in attendance. I had worked at New Directions for almost thirteen years at that time and though I didn't want to leave I could feel that my time was up there. I was out of work for about six months before landing a job with the Amity Foundation as a Case Manager. I left there in twenty nineteen and have been out of work except for a brief tenure as Program Manager for a new transitional living program. That job ended this past December, and I am contemplating retirement.

My brother Amos passed away last year from non-covid related illnesses. He died about a month before his sixty-second birthday. It hit me really hard, and I thought about how grateful I was to have visited him for a couple of weeks that summer before. Amos was an all-American guy. Handsome, a high school football star, who was awarded an academic scholarship at Perdue Universities School of Engineering. He worked a full-time job and was married with two boys but was still able to graduate from Perdue in five years. He went on to settle in Huntsville Alabama and worked in a nuclear power plant until he retired. My brother too was born at Ellsworth Air Force Base near Rapid City South

THE AMERICAN

Dakota. We used to joke all the time that the only other Black me that we knew of that was born in South Dakota was us. I miss him dearly. I write about Amos because his is the all-American Story that to this day is almost never told in the mainstreams of America when it comes to Black men. Bug grew up poor in the projects, played sports went to college worked hard, paid taxes, and bought a couple of houses. He was a regular member of his Church and a respected neighbor in his community. When he died, he was able to make sure that his five boys would be able to make a better life for themselves and their children. Amos realized that the surest way out of the hood was through education and hard work. Amos achieved the American dream and achieved it in the American way as have millions of Black men have done throughout the history of this country.

Today, like I am sure are all Americans, no matter what side you are on, I am concerned about the future of our country. It is my opinion that our elected federal officials, in the US House of Representatives and the US Senate are to blame for much of the unrest we see in American streets today. If the leaders of our country treat each other as enemies then so too will their followers. Partisanship cannot successfully govern and can only lead to division. From all appearances the Republican party seems

Anthony Belcher

to relish its role as the worst of the bad guys. The Republican party is all but openly saying they are the party of White people. While I wasn't surprised with the election of Donald Trump as the forty-fifth president, and agree his election was more about White Supremist backlash, or White American fears about being replaced at the top of the food chain in American society, I was surprised and terribly disappointed at how high-ranking members of the Republican party has allowed Mr. Trump and his minions to embarrass, shame, and rip off the country that we all claim to love. When Mr. Trump first announced his candidacy I too, was intrigued with the prospect of a successful businessman running the country. However, after conducting some research, it wasn't long before I was sure that he was a charlatan and would be a disaster for the country. I need to look no further than the events on January sixth, when a whole nation watched as the President of the United States assembled a mob and then sicked that mob on the US Capital to disrupt the confirmation of the votes making Joe Biden our forty-sixth president, to confirm that my concerns were warranted. A US president had called for an insurrection of the United States. The fact that the same US Senators, and Congresspeople who were cowered in the Capital Chambers, in fear of their lives, are now downplaying the event or denying there

THE AMERICAN

was an insurrection at all. Their actions are the most cowardly of any that I have ever witnessed in my lifetime. How can they expect that any rational person would support them after President Trump put their lives at risk, while the world watched, and they now say it didn't happen. Now they don't want to appoint a special commission to investigate and find out how something like that can happen so they can prevent it from happening again? Wow!

    I would remind all elected officials state, city, county, or otherwise that their job is to serve the "All American People" no matter what they look like or what they believe in. When our political leaders openly flame the minor divisions of our society, rather than work together to provide fair compromise to resolve these issues, then they can only lead us to disaster. Today our political landscape and the divisions in our society make me think that this must have been what it was like in the years and months that lead to the Civil War. If the Republican Party with all of its talk about conservative values, actually practiced this in principle they would find themselves as the multi-racial political party in America. Many Black and Brown people vote for the Democrats, not so much because of their politics, but for their inclusiveness, because Democrats appear to be offering a seat at the table of power to all Americans. I am in no way saying that the Democratic

Anthony Belcher

party does not have its own issues with how it has traditionally and continues to treat Americans of color, however, they seem to be the political party of all Americans. If this nation, the first and only of its kind in the history of the world is to survive, it will not be as it has in the past with White people being the main beneficiaries of the American Dream.

I have always thought that Black folks, the descendants of the American slave are indignant to this country. Like the Native American the descendant of the slave was created in and by America. While all of Europe was involved in the Atlantic Slave Trade, the fancy name attached when Europeans decided that all slaves should come from Africa, was responsible for enslaving millions of Africans and shipped them off to work in the Americas, which to Europeans was a new world. However, it is the descendants of the American Slave who over the last one hundred and fifty years that has made the most impact on the world. There is a reason that America's version of Beethoven, and Bach, are named Charlie, Duke, Miles, Dizzy, and Louie, just to name a few. Malcom X's "Ballot or the Bullet" speech is as much a passionate testimony for Americans desire for freedom as was Patrick Henry's "Give Me Liberty or Give Me Death" speech given some two hundred years before. Dr. King eloquently spoke of

The American

what the American Dream should be standing on the steps of the Lincoln Memorial on that summer day in nineteen-sixty-three. Our story, the rise of the American slave from being considered as chattel property, to hold the highest elected offices in the land. Is the greatest example of the resiliency of the human spirit in the history of the world. I believe that it is only in America that the Dukes, the Dizzy's Louie's, and Malcolm's could prosper and become the world-renowned giants of music that they were.

The progress Black folk have made in this country and the world came at a tremendous cost. The atrocities perpetrated against Black folks by White folks against Black people was at best ignored by Federal, state and local authorities, or at worst perpetrated by them. The progress made over the years has been painstakingly slow, and the heinous acts committed against Black folk by Whites are still far too frequent and go mostly unpunished up to this day. That said, change did and continues to come. Maybe with the conviction of Derek Chauvin, the police officer who murdered George Floyd signals the beginning of real change in how White police officers conduct themselves when dealing with Black citizens.

My birth certificate states Negro in the place that designates what race I belong to. Throughout my young life

Anthony Belcher

we referred to ourselves as Colored, or Black. To this day my mother will take offense to being called black as for many in her generation Colored was the preferred name. Calling someone Black back then was perceived as you calling them ugly. I have always preferred what I was known as in England which was the American. Not a Black American, just American. I don't protest the official "African American" moniker, that is mostly accepted as the best way to describe Black folk indignant to this country. I'm sure that in many ways it's a better description of Americans like me than "Colored" or "Negro". I actually prefer Black, (thanks James), I would love to feel again the way I did when I was referred to as the American in England. I would love to feel the hope I felt when I was a fifth grader reading the biographies of America's heroes.

Though it is clear to me that my story could not have happened anywhere else in the world but America. Unfortunately, I stopped feeling like I was an American that day in sixty-eight while watching Bull Conner and his dogs, and his billy clubs and his water hoses…. Or when I watch the George Floyds, Eric Gardeners, or Brianna Taylors die at the hands of the Bull Conners of today. Yet, and still, I proudly think of myself as an American and am equally proud of my Black heritage. I am descended to

THE AMERICAN

the Slave, a people who rose from bondage to hold the highest offices in this land.

Today I am retired after a twenty-year career working with homeless and addicted persons, particularly homeless veterans. I am a husband. I am a father my children can be proud of. I am a grandfather that spoils his grandchildren. I am a law-abiding citizen. I am a concerned member of my community. I am American. White America can no longer take that from me. I am no longer willing to allow them to.

> Truths that hurt will heal
> While lies will only fester
> Turning to old sores

www.ingramcontent.com/pod-product-compliance
Lightning Source LLC
Chambersburg PA
CBHW072149070526
44585CB00015B/1062